# A Brief History
## of
## Cryptology

# A Brief History
## of
# Cryptology

*J. V. Boone*

Naval Institute Press
Annapolis, Maryland

Naval Institute Press
291 Wood Road
Annapolis, MD 21402

Unless noted otherwise, all photos are from the collection of J. V. Boone.

ISBN-13: 978-1-59114-084-9

Library of Congress Cataloging-in-Publication Data

Boone, J. V.
    A brief history of cryptology / J.V. Boone.
        p. cm.
    Includes bibliographical references and index.
    ISBN 1-59114-084-6 (alk. paper)
    1. Telecommunication—Security measures.    2. Computer security.
3. Cryptography.    I. Title.
TK5102.85.B66 2005
005.8′2—dc22

                                                        2005000009

Printed in the United States of America on acid-free paper ∞
12  11  10  09  08  07            9  8  7  6  5  4  3  2

This work has been approved for publication by the National Security Agency history program. Its contents and conclusions are those of the author and contributors, based on their research, and do not necessarily represent the official views of the National Security Agency or the Department of Defense.

# CONTENTS

# FOREWORD

This book, in one easily accessible condensed form, tells the remarkable story of how encryption techniques have evolved through the centuries, and the even more remarkable story of how human ingenuity and computer technology have been used to decrypt ever more complex encrypted messages. Toward the end of his life, the Duke of Wellington said, "I've spent most of my career wondering what was on the other side of the hill." Indeed, all military leaders have based their tactics on their assumption as to the enemy's location and intent. Thus, maintaining secrecy has always been a vital part of any general's war planning, as has concomitantly attempting to uncover the secrets of his opponents. These two related objectives took on a dramatically different dimension and importance in the twentieth century as large quantities of military planning and operational data began to be transmitted over radios and telephones. The primary means of maintaining secrecy of radio and telephone conversations has been encryption, and, of course, the primary means of uncovering the secrets of these encrypted conversations has been decryption.

Decryption operations reached a zenith in World War II, when the American and British intelligence teams broke the codes being used by the Japanese and Germans and managed to keep this remarkable breakthrough a secret. As a result, both the German and Japanese military had their plans and operations revealed to Allied military, generally before they conducted the operations. It is no exaggeration to say that this intelligence breakthrough was a critical factor in the Allied victory, and, without question, prevented hundreds of thousands of casualties in the Allied military forces.

Today, radio communications have become substantially more pervasive than in World War II. And not just voice or telegraphic messages are being communicated, but facsimile data, graphical data, video data, and computer data. And these data are being transmitted worldwide by satellites and fiber-optic lines, both marine and terrestrial.

But as military forces become more and more dependent on radio and telephone communications, so also do they become more vulnerable to these communications being intercepted and interpreted. Thus, today we have the same two requirements we had in World War II—maintaining the secrecy of our communications and uncovering our opponents' secrets. But today it is even more technically challenging to succeed in these missions and more critically important that we do so.

This document, then, and the National Cryptologic Museum that inspired it should be seen both as a tribute to the remarkable achievements of intelligence teams of the past and as a challenge to intelligence teams of the future, from whom we will need even more remarkable achievements.

William J. Perry[1]

# PREFACE

Cryptology? Our research team uses this term to refer to the arts and sciences involved in protecting one's information from unintended recipients and also in exploiting information. The term has both defensive and offensive connotations. Practical needs for cryptology exist in many segments of today's information age and a colorful history has emerged associated with the technologies that have evolved to fill these needs, the people and organizations that have been active in the area, and the importance of some of the applications. Some of this history is presented in the National Cryptologic Museum.[1] This small yet unique museum attracts a wide spectrum of visitors. Some are experts in cryptology, but most are not. Most come to learn.

When we first took on this writing project, we intended to produce some introductory materials for the museum. Good museums have a mission of not only educating their visitors, but also provoking their curiosity. That worked for us. As we went about answering the many new questions we encountered, we were reminded that technical specialists tend to communicate only with each other. When they write, they often lean toward complex mathematical formulations. Nevertheless, we believed that we could find a middle ground between the mass of technical papers that describe the latest developments in complex technological adventures and a simple two-page brochure that people with a very wide variety of backgrounds and training can enjoy. This book is our effort to explore that middle ground. We trust that it will answer many questions and raise some new ones. We hope that this book will raise public awareness about the value of a solid national cryptologic program to keep our country secure and will encourage many younger professionals to join this important field.

As we say in chapter 1, our primary goal is to illustrate some of the technological history of the cryptologic arts and sciences by providing an historical overview of the technological development of communications and computers, and using that history to set the context for the technology that has been applied to cryptologic systems.

Our treatment of cryptography is largely intuitive; readers will find no equations in this book. Experts will perhaps find the treatment superficial, but we wish to reach a wider audience. However, we have included some material to provoke the experts. Because we use some terms that may not be familiar to everyone, we have provided a glossary and a variety of references, both old and new.

We have also learned a few things about historical research. As engineers and mathematicians, we generally prefer a rational and orderly thought process. Real life rarely fits this model. The complex interactions of people, business goals, academic pursuits, personalities, events, and sometimes irrational forces (war, for example) often force technological connections that would not otherwise occur. They sometimes break these connections too. Moreover, there are always many versions of what "really" happened. One of our friends, Maj. Gen. David D. Bradburn, USAF (Ret.), had recently completed a serious work of military history and advised, "Remember that as time goes on, people's memories become clearer and clearer about things that never happened!" We have tried to follow Dave's good advice as we developed the context for events and their associated technological developments.

In our quest for accuracy, we have drawn on our personal knowledge and consulted many references. A good many of these references have been reported in a variety of publications. As is typical for this type of work, we found that sometimes the references conflict with each other. Therefore, in addition to the endnotes, the bibliography lists references that are available for further study rather than a fact-by-fact listing of all sources. Obviously, we have avoided classified material; we believe an accurate understanding of the topic essentials and issues is possible with the available materials.

The overview in chapter 1 contains a condensed version of activities in World War II that illustrates the classic interaction of the three technology topics—communications, computers, and cryptology. In later chapters we repeat some of this material in more detail. We present chronologically intertwined descriptions of selected developments in the three fields. Our primary intent is to place the cryptologic arts and sciences in context with the developments in communications and computers. The evolution of cryptologic tools is integrated with the abridged timelines of the other fields. Photographs of key contributors and some important pieces of equipment are included. We have focused on "things" (meaning equipment or tools) and have chosen illustrations of the technologies in use in a given time period. The external view of a piece of equipment does not always fully reveal its internal technological complexity, but sometimes the object's size and a description of its capability adequately illustrate the path of technological development. The captions for the illustrations are designed to add to the in-text information. References are provided for those who wish to further investigate.

Because of the complexity of each field, we lay no claim as to the completeness of our presentation. However, we have attempted to select people, events, technological advancements, and particular equipment that illustrate the progress and circumstances fairly and accurately.

We thank the many people who assisted in this project. Dr. David Hatch and Col. W. J. Williams, USAF, the chiefs of the Center for Cryptologic History (CCH) during the course of our work, and Jack Ingram, historian and curator of the National Cryptologic Museum, deserve our special thanks. Daniel Wolf provided encouragement and support in important ways. We received excellent support and suggestions from many others but Dick Day, Jim Philbad, and Mort O'Connor were particularly great sources of information and assistance with facts, context, and content while Ann Caracristi, Bob Rich, Andrew Martinez, and Harry Hayes were special sources of advice and support. A particular thank you is given to David W. Gaddy, past chief of the CCH, for making an intriguing comment that sparked the idea of looking at cryptologic history in this particular way. All of these people were extremely helpful. The residual mistakes are ours.

This publication is dedicated to our respected friend and coworker Thomas Prugh, who died in April 2002 while this work was still in progress. His support and personal contributions are much appreciated. His short biography is included in the list of contributors at the end of the book. Tom was one of those who made some of the interactions actually occur!

# A Brief History
of
Cryptology

# 1

# OVERVIEW

Today, we routinely use the results of the combined technology advances in at least three fields—communications, computers, and cryptography.

In our daily lives, most of us experience the interactions of communications, computers, and cryptography in a very real way, often without even noticing. Other times, our attention is quite drawn to the way these systems interact. For example, when we make purchases over the Internet using our personal computers, we may encounter a standard notice as shown on page 2.

The communications path for our purchase may start out with cable connections, or it may be supported by wireless transmissions to the computer in our home or office. The communications network that connects us to the appropriate business may employ a combination of traditional telephone wires, cables, fiber-optic links, microwave relay systems, and satellite-borne relays. Populating the entire network are complex computer-like switches and routers, which ensure that the proper connectivity is established and maintained. The system automatically employs built-in cryptographic techniques that reduce the risk of unauthorized access to our personal data and provide positive identification of the participants. Today's implementation of the parts of the total process, though hardly seamless, is certainly practical and efficient. Further improvements are always on the way. Those who call this the information age have a good argument!

This spread of information-related technologies is, of course, not limited to the United States. A clear link between the application of technology to society

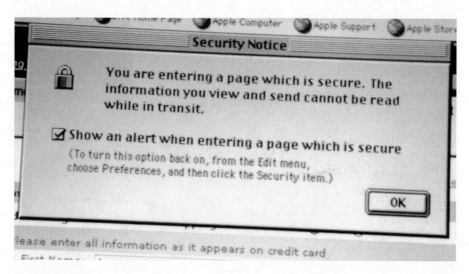

Typical Internet security notice. As this familiar notice reminds us, today's commercial encryption techniques are extremely useful in maintaining the privacy of personal and financial information. Financial institutions protect their activities with similar techniques.

and the ability of nations to improve their citizens' standard of living has emerged. An excellent summary of the situation follows: "Investment in technological improvement and in the complementary assets and activities needed to support innovation is a positive sum strategy for improving living standards."[1]

As living standards improve, sometimes the clash of the old and new is less than graceful. Cell phone users in restaurants, theaters, and other public locations have annoyed many of us. And visible evidence of the new technology can at times assault our sense of taste; at other times such evidence is quite visible, but we hardly notice it.

Because these technological innovations and applications are becoming increasingly important to all areas of society—including business, education, government, and finance—they will continue to expand. The critical investments come from many sources because the advancements are considered to be useful and worthwhile by many individuals and organizations.

The fields of communications, computers, and cryptography are more strongly connected than most may realize. As advances in technology affect more of us, interest in these interrelationships will increase. Understanding the history of all three technologies helps us see not only their economic challenges and benefits, but also their importance to our basic national security. Much has been said on

The meshing of old and new. In Cluny, France, a twelfth-century arch that held the doors to the world-famous abbey complex frames a twentieth-century, high-capacity satellite dish and a residential television antenna.

Office buildings are now supports for a wide variety of communications antennae. Almost any office building is now a platform for many communications systems. This illustration shows cellular phone antenna arrays and several types of public service radio systems that serve, for example, police and fire departments.

the importance of national intelligence activities, but it is difficult to improve on President Dwight D. Eisenhower's summary, which he presented while dedicating the headquarters building of the Central Intelligence Agency in November 1957: "In war nothing is more important to a commander than the facts concerning the strength, dispositions, and intentions of his opponent, and the proper interpretation of those facts. In peacetime the necessary facts are of a different nature. They deal with conditions, resources, requirements and attitudes prevailing in the world. They and their correct interpretation are essential to the development of policy to further our long term national security and best interests."

Cryptology has an important role to play in the intelligence activities of the nation. It is a crucial part of today's information age. Today, most of that information is in electronic form, but that was not always so.

As in the past, the proliferation of advanced technologies presents both challenges and opportunities to U.S. intelligence activities. The United States' superiority in cryptologic activities is an important factor in our overall national security. The National Cryptologic Museum presents some convincing evidence regarding the truth of that statement. Yet cryptology should not be viewed in isolation. It is, and always has been, closely linked to the evolution of communications and computer technology.

This book is intended to illustrate how the three fields of communications, computers, and cryptography have evolved together. The primary goal is to detail some of the technological history of cryptology by

- providing an historical overview of the technological development of communications and computers, and
- using that history to set the context for how that technology has been applied to cryptologic systems.

We include no detailed explanations as to how individual milestone accomplishments function or how they work (although some references will be provided for this purpose). The material concentrates on both how the developments have been intertwined and the current degree of interdependence among the three technologies.

It is an interesting story that we believe holds some clues about what the next steps may be. We intentionally approach the story from an intelligence and military command-and-control viewpoint. We chose that path because it is the one we know best. This less-known viewpoint and this story will add to the general understanding of the forces that have driven innovation and application of technology at the leading edges. For the purposes of illustration, the focus of this book is often on specific tools and equipment, but we realize that people and their ideas are the essential ingredients for true progress and success. To emphasize this point, we provide background information on key individuals as well as their organizational associations.

Cryptology remains a specialized, and at times exotic, topic, and its terminology and concepts are unfamiliar to many. A detailed knowledge of all of its complexities, however, is not necessary to understand cryptology's technological histories and their interrelationships. Appendix A presents a simplified, non-mathematical presentation on the subject so that readers can develop an intuitive feel for the topic. This treatment, while probably too elementary for some, will hopefully provoke in many readers a sense of curiosity and the desire for further study. Right now, the reader simply needs to know that cryptography is classically referred to as the science and study of secret writing. Understanding the following terms may also be helpful:

Plaintext is the original form of a message or set of data. Anyone who knows the language of the message (and has access to it) can read and understand it.

Ciphertext is the result of the cryptographic process of encipherment. The intent of the process is to make the original message unintelligible to anyone but the intended recipients.

Cryptographic key is the piece, or pieces, of information that allows the intended recipients to read the enciphered message by means of decipherment. They must also know the method of encipherment.

Transmission is the method of delivering the message or data from one party to another.

Interception is the process used by an unintended recipient to gain access to a message or data set (whether in ciphertext or not).

Cryptography is the general term used to describe the arts and sciences of securing messages by encryption. People who do this are called cryptographers.

Cryptanalysis is the general term used to describe the arts and sciences used by unintended recipients for recovering plaintext from ciphertext. The men and women who do this are called cryptanalysts.

Again, the term "cryptology" involves all of the above terms and has both defensive and offensive connotations. Some definitions of cryptology are broader than ours. They usually include techniques and systems that are used to intercept (or collect) the information as well as many of the activities associated with extracting intelligence information from non-communications signals (such as those associated with radar and instrumentation). These issues, though interesting and important, are beyond the scope of this work.

We will also use and describe some additional terms as they occur. Two in particular are "codes" and "ciphers." Many references use them interchangeably, which can be misleading. The differences between these two terms are mentioned in appendix A.

## Technological Imperatives Drive All Three Fields

Advances in one field drive advances in another. No matter where the motivation for technological advancement comes from—government, industry, or the powerful drive of the high-technology marketplace—those responsible for the cryptologic capability of a nation must obtain and apply the latest techniques. This challenge is continuing. History shows that second place status in either cryptography or cryptanalysis is unacceptable!

While communications and computational capability are not the only areas that have driven the cryptologic fields, they have the strongest influence since they are naturally imbedded in the process of secure communications. Of obvious importance to the success of cryptology is recording and data storage technology, as well as advanced mathematical capability, which is absolutely essential. Extensive knowledge of linguistics is another essential ingredient in the total cryptologic mix of talent and technology. Although communications and computer development are benchmarks for the cryptologic timeline we presented, the greatest gain for the nation lies in the timely ability to place these technologies in the system context of the cryptologic problems. This holds true for the problem of protecting our own information or of uncovering the capabilities and intentions of an adversary.

Demands for higher speed and increased bandwidth affect cryptographers (code makers) and drive them to use advanced technology. However, it is the cryptanalyst (code breaker) who has an insatiable need for advances in computer technologies. The interactions between communications and computer technologies are very powerful. In the field of cryptology, the nations with the most advanced technologies have a clear and distinct advantage over all others. This important point has serious import-export policy implications as governments try to obtain a balanced national security policy.[2]

This situation is hardly new. Nations have always applied useful innovations rapidly, and these innovations have demanded both political and technical responses. In turn, a nation's ability to respond to technology advances depends on innovative people and how they use the latest tools. One country takes a step that forces others to also change. In this sense, the nations are not completely in charge of their own programs. Even with the best technology, people are the key factor to success.

The cycles continue. The complex motivations that drive the leading-edge developments in cryptographic systems can make the change process chaotic.

Historians get a mere glimpse of the factors involved in this exciting technology that has often played a crucial role in history. The amazing progress brought about by the challenges of World War II is one such example.

## The Example of World War II[3]

The end of World War II saw the wide use of telegraphy and the worldwide expansion of telephonic and radio communications. Secure governmental or business communications were achieved manually. No means of communicating securely by voice were available; however, it was clear to many that only through advances in cryptography would the potential for advancements in communications techniques be realized. Many individuals and organizations were engaged in this goal, but probably none had more impact than a German engineer named Arthur Scherbius. In the early 1920s he invented and patented an electromechanical machine for rapidly encrypting written messages. Although originally intended for business purposes, this machine, the ENIGMA, was adopted by the German government in the mid-1920s and became one of the principal cryptographic tools of that country for the next two decades. Not only was it faster than previous techniques, but it produced sophisticated ciphertext. It presented a serious challenge to anyone who wished to listen in on German military and governmental matters.

The Polish government was well aware of its need to listen in and was fortunate to gain the services of three mathematicians, Jerzy Rozycki, Henryk Zygalski, and Marian Rejewski, who took on the task of analyzing the products of the ENIGMA machine, which by the early 1930s were appearing in a variety of forms. This brilliant threesome, with help from Polish industry, developed the tools and procedures to exploit ENIGMA traffic until late 1938, when new technical changes were introduced. The Polish team moved to France, where they continued their work with French help. In mid-1939, they also assisted a British team of cryptographers from Bletchley Park.

In mid-1938 Bletchley Park had become the location of the group of British (and later, American) cryptographers who were attacking ENIGMA and other cipher systems. A principal investigator was mathematician Alan Turing. Turing built on the work of the Polish and French teams, added unique innovations of his own, and by late 1939 had developed the specifications for an elaborate electromechanical device, called the BOMBE, which was used to analyze ENIGMA ciphertext and recover the key settings of the machine. Eventually, hundreds of the BOMBEs, in several versions, were manufactured and used in both England and the United States. In the United States, the National Cash Register Company was the major producer; in the United Kingdom, the British

Tabulating Machine Company dominated. This combined effort permitted selected ENIGMA decryptions to be produced regularly within hours of their original transmission. There is no question that this capability played an important part in shortening the war.

Behind this remarkable accomplishment was a huge supporting infrastructure of intercept stations, secured communications, punch-card data processing machines, and other technologies that were in public use at the time. Of particular interest on the cryptographic side, the U.S. Army and Navy had both adopted an electromechanical encryption machine called SIGABA, or Mark II ECM.

The World War II SIGABA, or ECM, cryptographic machine of the United States. This imposing electromechanical machine was not only innovative, but also highly secure and saw wide use in World War II. It was the first such piece of equipment to be used by both the Army and the Navy, permitting secure communications between cooperating forces. *Center for Cryptologic History*

This highly advanced machine was produced by the Teletype Corp. and was based on a design by William Friedman and Frank Rowlett. Extraordinary effort had succeeded in placing these machines in deployed operation by mid-1941 (SIGABA was never broken by any World War II power). Although the Allies had the information advantage, there was more to be done.

There were other cryptographic systems used by Germany. One of the most challenging was called TUNNY. While also electromechanical in nature, it was far more complex than ENIGMA. Even the newest electromechanical analytical tools were far too slow for the cryptanalysts. An engineer in the British Post Office, Tommy Flowers, took the lead and designed, developed, and built a computing machine called COLOSSUS. Although it was designed specifically for cryptanalysis, this vacuum-tube electronic machine was the first program-controlled electronic digital computer. Built in the amazingly short time of about seven months, it was tested and placed in operation in late 1943. There was even more to come!

The officials of the United States and the United Kingdom needed to be able to speak to each other securely. Written communications, then as today, were no replacement for human conversation. Fortunately, the technical groundwork for a solution was in place at the Bell Telephone Laboratories (BTL).[4] Key elements of a digital voice synthesizer that reconstructed intelligible voice sounds from digital input signals had been demonstrated at the 1939 World's Fair in New York. BTL engineers including Ralph Potter, Homer Dudley, Harry Nyquist, and Claude Shannon designed an advanced electronic system that included a new method of data encoding called Pulse Code Modulation (along with several other "firsts" in communications technology). The system was a success, and when it was put in use in mid-1943, it became the first realization of enciphered telephony. By the end of the war, terminals were installed at many locations around the world and remained in use during the critical postwar period.

In his foreword to this book, Dr. Perry has noted the extremely important role that cryptologic superiority played in the Allied victory in World War II. The technological developments that enabled that superiority came very rapidly. In a very short period of time, about twenty years, cryptographic and cryptanalytic techniques and the equipment to support them had moved from what was essentially a paper-and-pencil process, through an electromechanical phase, and ended with the development of the electronic digital computer, digital telephony, and the true beginnings of the current digital age. This accomplishment was the result of advancements in mathematics, communications techniques for both data and voice, and an extended set of applications of state-of-the-art information storage and processing technologies. It had involved at least six governments (both friend and foe), universities, government organizations, and a wide variety of industries in several countries. Although the threat of war and the war itself sparked these intense activity levels, the story was far from over.

The cycles of interaction continue today.

## A Look Ahead

In this book, we present three highly interrelated technologies (communications, computers, and cryptology) and the chronological events surrounding them. In some cases, advances in communications have provoked advances in cryptography. In other cases, cryptanalytic demands have brought about technological advances in computing. Advances in fundamental work in mathematics and electronic technology have driven all three areas. We will highlight specific technology developments that have affected several advances in significant ways.

The pace of progress is not uniform. As we have seen, World War II forged progress in many areas in a relatively short period of time. As the driving forces change to, for example, those driven by economic and trade considerations, the pace of progress varies widely. As we consider the future it is difficult to predict where the next major driving force will emerge and which technical advancement will support it. The only clear lesson that we can glean from history: anyone who assumes that these fields will see no further major advances is quite mistaken.

Technical leadership in any of these related fields, including cryptology, is sometimes based in government, sometimes in the university setting, and sometimes in industry. This fact is an important factor in the evolution of today's global information technology industries. The fundamental international nature of these industries and their intellectual base means that the future relationships between governments and their industries are more important than ever before; they are certainly as complex as at any time in history.

You are encouraged to use your imagination as you examine what was, guess what might have been, and ponder what can be.

All three fields remain exciting today!

# 2

## 1200–1800:
## THE INTRODUCTION
## OF MECHANICAL AIDS

Why choose this period (circa 1200–1800) to begin a narrative about the technologies of communications, computers, and cryptology?

Important events in every area of human activity occurred in this period of civilization. One could start a narrative here on just about any subject. However, some particular technology developments of these times will set the stage for the progress to be discussed in the following chapters. This extended period of history contains time segments described in such grand terms as the Age of Discovery, the Reformation, the Enlightenment, and similar names. The impressive names of these eras are merited. Consider the following condensed list of now-famous people and events that belong to this six-hundred-year period:

The Venetian merchant Marco Polo (1254–1324) travels the Silk Road of commerce and writes of the riches and wonders of the Asian world. His stories have great influence on the European population and the events of these times.

The sailor-explorer Christopher Columbus (1451–1506), a native of Genoa, Italy, who gained most of his seafaring experience sailing for Portugal, lands in the New World in 1492 and claims it for his sponsors, the king and queen of Spain.

The Prussian scientist and astronomer Nicolaus Copernicus (1473–1543) makes some fundamental observations about the nature of the solar system.

The Portuguese sea captain Ferdinand Magellan (1480–1521), sailing for the king of Spain, sets out in 1519 on what will be the first circumnavigation of the earth, a voyage that is finished under the command of Juan Sebastián del Cano who, along with only seventeen others of the original five-ship crew of 236, completed the entire trip in 1522.[1]

The German Martin Luther (1483–1546) and the Frenchman John Calvin (1509–1564) are principals of the Protestant Reformation of the Christian church and have great indirect impact on European society in general.

The Italian Galileo Galilei (1564–1642) invents the telescope and presents to the public more fundamental observations about the nature of the solar system.

The British establish a colony in what will become known as Jamestown, Virginia, in 1607.

The English scientist and mathematician Isaac Newton (1642–1727) makes fundamental contributions to what we now call physics and mathematics.

America declares its independence from Britain in 1776.

The French storm the Bastille in Paris in 1789.

Even this abbreviated list reveals that these were exciting times. The events often involved communications, calculations (if not computers), and sometimes even cryptologic activities. At the start of this period, all functions in any of these three categories were accomplished manually and typically in pen and ink.

Early in this general period the literate segment of the society in the West began to use numerals and numbers in general practice. To appreciate the interaction of mathematics with communications, it is helpful to understand the origin of the number system that we use today. David Smith and Jekuthiel Ginsburg summarize the start of the process:

We do not know how long ago it was that human beings first began to make their thoughts known to one another by means of speech, but it seems probable that people learned to use words in talking many thousands of years before they learned to set down these words in writing. In the same way, after people learned to name numbers it took a long time for them to learn to use signs for the numbers; for example, to use the numeral "2" instead of the word "two."

Where and when did the use of numerals begin? This question takes us back to the very beginnings of history. If you look at a map you will see Egypt, lying along the valley of the Nile. As long ago as 3000 BC—perhaps even earlier—there were prosperous cities with markets and business houses, and with an established government over all the land. The commercial and government records necessitated the use of large numbers. So the Egyptians made up a set of numerals by which they could express numbers of different values from units up to hundreds of thousands.[2]

With this start, and later efforts in India, Greece, and Roman societies, a system of numbers had evolved in Europe about the year 1200. Today we call these Arabic numbers, but they would be more properly called Hindu-Arabic because they were based on an Indian manuscript on arithmetic that was translated into Arabic and then into Latin. This complex story remains unclear, but what is clear is that these concepts of numbers, including the important concept of "zero," did take hold in Europe and provided the basis for arithmetic and mathematics work in that part of the world. We talk of globalization today, but it is not new! The first entry in our technological timeline will be written as

## Circa 1200 AD

Arabic numbering systems were in use in Europe.

Although literacy was by no means widespread, manuscripts were relatively common and an early form of printing that involved woodcuts was in use. However, it took a long time to produce a book or even a short document. In addition to the labor involved, the materials used in the writing and printing processes were expensive. Will Durant summarized the situation in his epic work *The Story of Civilization* by noting:

> Writing was upon parchment, papyrus, vellum, or paper, with quill or reed pens using black or colored inks. Papyrus disappeared from common use in Europe after the Islamic conquest of Egypt. Vellum, prepared from the skin of young lambs, was expensive, and was reserved for luxurious manuscripts. Parchment, made from coarse sheepskin, was the usual medium of medieval writing. Until the twelfth century paper was a costly import from Islam; but in 1190 paper mills were set up in Germany and France, and in the thirteenth century Europe began to make paper from linen.[3]

As the supply of affordable paper increased and access to education increased, the flow of written communications spread rapidly. Business, church, and government records also expanded as a part of the overall process of the developing commerce. The exact cause and effect is probably not known, but soon the first computational aid was seen in Asia. This leads to our second timeline entry.

## Circa 1300 AD

The abacus, beads strung on wires or rods and mounted in a frame, is in use in China. While it is technically an aid in counting, rather than a calculator, it proves to be a useful mechanical aid for maintaining business accounts. It is a great improvement over its predecessor, the counting boards, and versions of it remain in use today.

New techniques, rather than new tools, tended to dominate the next four hundred years of progress, but a few important tools were developed and introduced.

In the early 1450s the German Johannes Gutenberg (1397–1468) developed a printing press that used moveable type. This advance in technology took advantage of the availability of paper and improvements in ink and provided a foundation for a publishing industry. Gutenberg and his fellow inventors and businessmen provided the fundamental tools, but marketing and sales techniques were required to ensure its widespread use. It took time, but it did happen.

No matter whether a message was handwritten or printed, whether it was expensive or cheap, or whether it was personal or related to government or business, someone had to physically transport it between the author/publisher and the reader. Human communication over long distances remained tied to physical transportation capabilities.

The process of transporting messages, regardless of the purpose, can expose the message contents to unintended recipients. The Egyptians and others recognized this danger long before the advent of the printing press, which led to very early use of cryptographic techniques. The expanding commerce of the time and increasing use of written communications were some of the factors that led to developments in cryptologic tools and techniques. This process has always been an interactive one.

The tools of the cryptologic arts and sciences draw from, and sometimes provoke, leading-edge developments in communications and computation.

In his book *The Codebreakers*,[4] historian David Kahn presents what he terms "The Pageant of Cryptology." It is indeed a pageant, one that includes colorful people, exotic ideas, intrigue, and an evolving set of tools. Kahn's work is a classic; here we will concentrate on only some of the tools and their characteristics. Although people remain the most vulnerable part of any secure method of communicating, the tools and the ideas behind them are essential elements.

## Circa 1466

The Italian Renaissance man Leon Battista Alberti (1406–1472) described the cipher disk and presented a method of using it that became known as polyalphabetic substitution.

His cipher disk consisted of two concentric disks of differing diameters, joined at their centers in a way that permitted them to rotate relative to each other. The circumference of each disk was divided into twenty-four equal parts that he called cells. The cells of the inner disk contained twenty-four letters of the Latin alphabet, but in a randomized order. The cells on the larger, or outside disk each contained one of twenty letters of the Latin alphabet in their normal order and then the numbers 1 to 4. To use the tool one first determined how to index the two rotating disks relative to each other and then read the ciphertext letters from the inside disk directly across from the plaintext letters on the outside disk. This process achieved encipherment. Alberti's process would, after every three or four words, re-index the disks, thereby creating the polyalphabetic cipher. Decipherment was accomplished by first indexing the disks in the same manner and then recovering the plaintext from the outside cells adjacent to the cells of the received ciphertext. Alberti also used the cipher disk to encrypt predetermined codes.

While both the author of the message and the recipient needed to have identical disks and an understanding of the rules for the progressive indexing, this deceptively simple tool made the encryption and decryption processes much faster and more reliable than they had been. The polyalphabetic cipher and the use of enciphered codes were also big steps forward.

David Kahn calls Alberti the Father of Western Cryptology. Versions of his innovative cipher disk were used in serious applications for over four hundred years and are still seen today, sometimes as the logo of cryptologic activities and organizations.

## 1518

*Polygraphia*, the first printed book on cryptography, was published in Germany. The multitalented abbot and author, Johannes Tritemius (1462–1516), added the technique of changing the key at every letter in a progressive manner, which delayed the repetition of the key and added significant complexity to the job of cryptanalysis. His method of presenting the progressively shifted alphabets in an orderly set of rows and columns, or a tableau, could be considered his contribution to technological tools. It has remained useful to this day.

## 1550

Girolamo Cardano (1501–1575), a leading mathematician and physician in Milan, Italy, developed and published the idea of "autokey." That is the use of the plaintext as a key to encipher itself and then starting over with each new plaintext word. Although implementing his concept met with serious flaws, the basic idea was a good one. He made other contributions, one of which led to a tool that consisted of a perforated mask that could be placed over a blank page. The originator of the message to be secured would write it, word or phrase at a time, through the various openings in the mask and then fill in the remainder of the page with another, uninvolved, message that incorporated the secret text. All correspondents needed identical masks, and this technique required skill and ingenuity. However, this tool did find a limited market for a considerable amount of time.

## 1586

Blaise de Vigenère (1523–1596) of France made many contributions to cryptography and the associated literature, but perhaps his most important contribution is his improvement of the autokey system by adding the use of a "priming" key. This was a formidable technique and is still the basis of some systems today. It did not require any new physical tools. He also created another new, and actually less secure, enciphering technique that carries his name today. This technique uses a tableau of cipher alphabets, each row shifted one space to the left of the one above it. The columns and rows are each indexed by a normal alphabet. Correspondents must share a keyword. The sender creates ciphertext by using the tableau in combination with the keyword stream, and the receiver reverses the process to recover plaintext. (See appendix A for an illustration of this type of polyalphabetic system.)

Of course, all of these techniques and their many variants were limited to the transport of written material between the correspondents. Among those items that needed to be transported was the "key." If several parties lacked the key and a shared understanding of how the systems worked, all were forced into the role of the cryptanalyst. The systems were slow, somewhat awkward to use, and unforgiving of errors.

Progress continued in the field of mathematical calculation.

## 1673

Gottfried Wilhelm von Leibniz's (1646–1716) calculator mechanized both multiplication and addition. Born in Poland, Leibniz was well known in most of Europe and was interested in a wide variety of technical topics.

## Mid- to Late-1700s

By this time the Europeans and others had developed many intriguing codes and ciphers and had taken steps to accommodate them into their governmental organizational structures. The American revolutionaries had only rather primitive cryptologic tools, and they were in the hands of amateurs. For example, when Lt. Gen. George Washington was presented with a suspicious encrypted letter in 1775, he was obliged to turn to three members of the Continental Army who were willing to take on the cryptanalytic task. The three, Reverend Samuel West, a Massachusetts chaplain, and the team of Elbridge Gerry, who was to become the fifth vice president of the United States, and Col. Elisha Porter of the Massachusetts Militia were successful against the substitution cipher that included a mixture of Greek, Latin, and other symbols. These two groups produced identical deciphered texts of the letter from Dr. Benjamin Church Jr. Dr. Church was a respected Boston physician, but the contents of the letter convinced Washington that Church was acting as a spy for the British.[5]

Washington became very skilled in matters of intelligence and became personally involved in the tradecraft of the cryptography of the times. As Dr. Ralph Weber summarizes the situation: "General Washington knew how to obtain special intelligence and, as importantly, how to mask it in dispatches. His thoughtful, thorough, and creative instructions reflected experience and practical knowledge on espionage practices, and especially secret writing. Facing an enemy that had overwhelming military power, Washington recognized the crucial necessity for intelligence and secrecy, for they promised military success and, as well, the continued independence of a new nation."[6]

After the war, Washington and others remained involved in maintaining the privacy of official communications. In addition, they took steps to ensure that private communications would also be protected from illegal access. This concern is clearly addressed in the ordinance for regulating the U.S. Post Office, which was published in 1782.[7] These regulations clearly defined the conditions under which the mail could be delayed or opened by governmental authorities. Although these particular rules have been frequently modified to bring practices into line with the technologies and practices of the times, the basic principles still stand today. Tampering with the mail is still a federal offense. The law remains an important tool for protecting the privacy of communications and information.

## Circa 1790

Thomas Jefferson, the multitalented U.S. secretary of state at this time, in cooperation with Robert Patterson of the University of Pennsylvania, invented a "wheel cipher" wherein thirty-six wheels, each with alphabetical symbols individually mixed and inscribed around the circumference, were placed on a common axle. When each correspondent had an identical cylinder and the wheels were identically aligned, a plaintext message enciphered by one could be read by the other.

For some reason Jefferson did not seem to use his wheel cipher, but he had a fundamental and clear appreciation of the value of encryption in both private and governmental communications. He and his fellow Virginians, James Monroe, James Madison, and Edmund Randolph, made significant use of an approxi-

"Wheel cipher" equipment circa 1790. This device, on display at the National Cryptologic Museum, may have belonged to President Thomas Jefferson. It implements the technique described in his papers. This particular device was clearly intended to be used with
the French language. *Center for Cryptologic History*

mately 1,700-unit code invented by Randolph. These codes replaced words, or
segments of words, by predetermined numbers. They led to an updated version of
a diplomatic code in 1803 that came to be known as the Monroe Cypher. Monroe and Robert L. Livingston used it to communicate with the United States during negotiations for the Louisiana Purchase and it remained in use for many
years.[8] Jefferson also provided a version of a Vigenère cipher to Meriwether Lewis
and William Clark for their historic explorations with the Corps of Discovery.

While official codes and ciphers were in use within governments and the basic
tools remained those of paper, pen, and ink, some important mechanical aids
were being developed.

Soon, technology would permit the separation of communications from transportation, and complex calculations would become mechanized.

# 3

# 1800–1895:
# THE INTRODUCTION OF THE
# TELEGRAPH, THE TELEPHONE,
# AND MECHANICAL
# COMPUTING AIDS

The development of the capability to "compute" followed the application of mathematics to increasingly complex problems.

On one hand, computers are simply devices that people use to perform calculations. On the other hand, they are much more; they have enabled us to do more than we would ever have been able to imagine without them. They did not simply spring into existence and, of course, they are still in the early stages of development.

The development of today's computing capability depended on advances in mathematics, solid-state physics, electronics, manufacturing processes, and innovative business and economic practices. The process continues today. As in the past, progress depends on the ideas and abilities of remarkable individuals who seem to thrive on solving difficult problems. Almost by definition, cryptographers and cryptanalysts deal with some of the most difficult mathematical and computational problems that the human mind can create. Therefore, they have always displayed an astounding appetite for the very latest in computational capability. Their demands have helped shape the history of computing and will no doubt help shape the future of computing as well.

It is perhaps too soon to be able to look back and confidently point to all of the crucial events that led to today's computing capability, but the following list of selected events highlights important steps in the process. Even in this concise list of events, you will see an extraordinary business dynamic at work. Whether or not the companies still exist, their contributions endure.

## *Early 1800s*

The Industrial Revolution was largely brought about by the application of mechanical devices to many types of work. Some of these applications would have major implications in areas other than their original field. For example, in 1803, the French weaver Joseph-Marie Jacquard began to work on an automatic loom using punched cards to store essential information. His successful invention made a serious contribution to the Industrial Revolution. His punch-card method of storing data became a standard tool in computational devices for more than a hundred years.

The cryptographers and cryptanalysts of this time period were still bound to the basic tools of the cipher disk and to some extent the wheel cipher described in chapter 2. Nevertheless, they continued to make major contributions to important national activities. A good example is that of George Scovell, an officer of the British Army who served under Gen. Arthur Wellesley, the Duke of Wellington. Scovell was frequently successful at deciphering captured enciphered messages of the army of Portugal and also messages using the higher-level Great Paris Cipher (or the Grand Chiffre). His work granted Wellington great strategic advantage over Napoleon's forces.[1] This lesson should remain clear: never underestimate what talented individuals can do with just pen and ink! And soon—with the advanced tools that were to emerge—they would be able to do even more.

Computing by machine was introduced, and a new era began.

## *1822*

The English inventor Charles Babbage produced the first model of his difference engine. Two of his objectives were to improve the accuracy of and to reduce the labor required to produce mathematical tables. By mechanizing the mathematical technique of "finite differences," he produced a way to calculate polynomials that could then be used to determine a wide variety of functions. Laborious calculations would be replaced by setting up his machine and actually turning a crank. His model worked, and he set out to construct an improved version on a much grander scale. Doron Swade of the London Science Museum observes: "The significance of the machine being automatic cannot be overstated. By cranking a handle, that is by exerting a physical force, you could for the first time achieve results that up to that point in history could only have been arrived at by mental effort-thinking. It was the first attempt of externalise a faculty of thought in an inanimate machine."[2]

Despite its elegant and practical concept, for a variety of reasons the full-scale machine was never completed. Although Babbage invested his own funds in his efforts, he also depended on government support, which eventually stopped.

A portion of Difference Engine No. 1, 1832. Babbage's computing equipment was almost entirely lost over the years. This photograph is of a portion of his original design. The mechanical complexity required precision-machining of many parts in a time when mass production was not fully available. A team at the London Science Museum, working from Babbage's original designs of 1847–49, produced a working model of his "Difference Engine No. 2" in 1991. It was much more capable and efficient than the 1832 version.
*Science and Society Picture Library of the London Science Museum*

However, Babbage continued to produce detailed designs for a machine that would not only perform the calculations, but also produce automatically the printed results in the desired form. Humans would only be required to set up the machine. Although his designs were marvels, he would not see them implemented in his lifetime.

As an adjunct to this story, in 1843 an article appeared by Augusta Ada, Countess of Lovelace, "Sketch of the Analytical Engine," which described Babbage's work and included some of her own analysis. Many believe that certain concepts of modern programming stem from this article, although this is a matter of some debate. Few disagree, however, about the fact that her article was an accurate account of Babbage's work that provided publicity for the potential of automatic computing as seen at that time.

The separation of human communication from transportation became a major trend in the mid-1800s.[3] Humans have probably always wanted to communicate over longer and longer distances. We simply have things to say, information to exchange, and ideas to share. The spoken word was the only reliable way to communicate until the advent of writing permitted the physical transportation of messages among people. Next, the printing press made it possible to increase the size of the audience. Various methods of visually communicating over distances (e.g., signal fires, flags, lamps, and even the optical telegraph of the late 1700s) were developed and exploited despite obvious restrictions on their use. However, it was not until the advent of electrical telegraphy that routine, timely communication over long distances became a major factor in the conduct of personal, industrial, military, and political affairs.

We describe here some of the major events in electronics and engineering that promoted this dramatic change in human interaction along with some indicators of usage, a few important standards, some business dynamics, and governmental regulatory actions. They are divided into interacting stages to provide emphasis on particular capabilities.

The invention of telegraphy started the modern communications revolution. The word *telegraphy* was derived from Greek with the loose meaning of *writing in distance*. The communicators were, at least at first, connected by wires.

## May 24, 1844

Samuel F. B. Morse demonstrated his telegraph system between Baltimore, Maryland, and Washington, DC. He not only demonstrated the basic process of signaling over distance, but also developed a method of sending the alphabetic symbols and numerals by means of a mixture of short and long "on" signals—the Morse code.

Samuel F. B. Morse (1791–1872). Samuel Morse was one of America's most talented portrait painters when he conceived of his invention. He received his patent in 1837 and
pressed on with demonstrations that culminated in his successful transmission of the message, "What Hath God Wrought!" from Baltimore, Maryland, to Washington, DC. This
illustration is from a daguerreotype made in the studio of the soon to be famous Mathew
Brady sometime between 1844 and 1860. It is one of the first such pictures made in America. Morse had met Daguerre while he was studying art in Paris and was one of the first
people in America to use the technique for portraits. *Library of Congress*

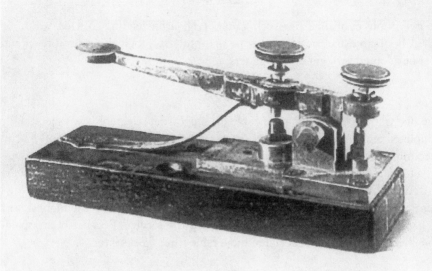

Morse telegraph key, circa 1845. This early telegraph key contains some improvements to the original that were designed and implemented by Alfred Vail, Morse's partner. *Smithsonian Institution*

The Morse code consists of short and long periods of electrical transmission called "dots" and "dashes" in predetermined patterns. The patterns represent all of the letters in the alphabet and the numerals one to nine plus zero. The selected representation for the alphabet has been cleverly assigned. The human sender controls the duration of the signal (short dots and longer dashes) and the human receiver interprets these as audible tones. The rate of transmission using Manual Morse averages only a few tens of five-character words per minute. The capacity of the transmission is limited, and the code is cleverly selected to maximize the rate of transfer based on how frequently the characters occur in the English language. The most efficient usage would be to assign the shortest code representations to the most frequently used characters. Morse noted that the most frequently used characters are E, T, and A. The dot, the shortest symbol, is assigned to the letter E; the second-shortest symbol, the dash, to the letter T; the dot-dash to the letter A; and so on.[4]

This original code, and many variants, is still in use today. Appendix A provides a brief discussion of the distinction between codes and ciphers.

# 1854

George Boole published his work, *Laws of Thought,* leading to what would be called Boolean Algebra. His rules for manipulating logical expressions would later be adopted by computer designers.

# 1858

The first transatlantic submarine cable for supporting telegraphy was successfully completed on August 5, 1858, after several failures. The previous attempts had all encountered breaks in the cable. This adventurous endeavor required the use of two steam-powered ships. The American *Niagara* and the British *Agamemnon* started in the mid-Atlantic and steamed in opposite directions toward Newfoundland and Ireland. The first transmission, "Glory to God in the highest, and on earth, peace, good will to men," launched the service. Because of an operational error, the cable was declared inoperable three weeks later.

# 1860

The commercial manufacture of keys began, and the telegraph industry, led by Western Union Co., expanded.

# 1861–65

The telegraph was used extensively in the conduct of the U.S. Civil War and helped to revolutionize the command-and-control aspects of warfare. Although signal flags and other methods of communications were also used, the telegraph provided a new capability, which was met with quick acceptance. Gen. Ulysses S. Grant wrote in his memoirs: "No order ever had to be given to establish the telegraph. The moment troops were in position to go into camp, the men would put up their wires." Gen. William Tecumseh Sherman also noted: "The value of the telegraph cannot be exaggerated, as illustrated by the perfect accord of action of the armies of Virginia and Georgia."

The Civil War in the United States brought about many changes in the command and control of military forces. All manner of communication techniques were in use including signal flags, heliographs, written materials, and the quickly maturing telegraph. There was a clear need for communications security, but little in the way of equipment to encourage its use. Most of the encryption systems in use were polyalphabetic substitutions and simple word transpositions. There was wide use, on both the Union and Confederate sides, of codebooks and cipher wheels. The Confederates also used a type of cipher reel that was a mechanized way to implement a Vigenère polyalphabetic system. Communications operators

Civil War headquarters field-telegraph station, 1864. This photograph shows the operator at the left of the picture with the telegraph key on his lap working outside of his tent-office. The wagon at right is a battery wagon that contained the power sources and other equipment for the line. It could also be used as a cramped office. The Photographic History of the Civil War (*New York: The Review of Reviews Co., 1912*), *vol. 8*

were well aware of the demands of these general types of systems; a single error in transmission might require that the entire message be retransmitted. They invented many ways to ensure the quality of their work. One Signal Corps operator, Sgt. Edwin Hawlely, developed a set of twenty-six wooden tablets, each with a different ciphertext alphabet; the set was intended to be used with a keyword. This invention received the first U.S. patent for a cipher device.[5]

While the telegraph was a new tool for long-distance communications, a tactical "line of sight" visual system had been put into operation prior to the start of the war. Its inventor was the army surgeon Albert James Myer (for whom Fort Myer, Virginia, is named). The system used a single flag (red square on white, or white square on red, depending on the background of the terrain), which was "wig-wagged" from side to side in a type of binary code. A crossed set of such flags is the insignia of the Army Signal Corps today. Since intercepting messages appeared relatively easy, the Union Army integrated the use of cipher disks and frequently changing codes into their flag signaling practices. The Confederates

Civil War field-telegraph station, 1864. Located at Wilcox Landing, this station is typical of the type of field installation that Grant's forces used to connect headquarters to brigades and/or divisions. The field line was made of rubber-coated wires, which were strung from a variety of objects and simply laid across fields. The stations were staffed by a combination of civilian and military personnel. The Photographic History of the Civil War (*New York: The Review of Reviews Co., 1912*), *vol. 8*

also used similar techniques. In fact, one of Myer's assistants from pre-war days, Edward Porter Alexander, had become involved with establishing the signaling system for the Confederacy.[6]

There were two major types of telegraph equipment used in the Civil War: a system called the Beardslee, and one based on Samuel Morse's equipment. While both systems had their technical problems, the real issue was one of technical incompatibility, which led to some complex organizational and management issues. This general type of problem continues today as technological variants acquire advocates with differing goals and objectives. Then as now, there is no easy answer. Nevertheless, the use of the telegraph in both strategic and tactical situations was an important innovation that affected the command and control of deployed forces.[7]

Confederate cipher reel. This reel was a mechanization of the Vigenère system of polyalphabetic substitution. This rare artifact of the U.S. Civil War was sent to the chief signal officer in Washington as a trophy after it was captured at Mobile, Alabama. The use of a tool such as this improved both the speed and accuracy of encryption and decryption processes. It is on display at the National Cryptologic Museum.

The heavy use of strategic and tactical communication by both sides, accentuated by the fact that each side knew the strengths and weaknesses of the other's communications techniques, led to many attempts at signals exploitation for military purposes. Today's "information warfare" advocates can find examples of almost every aspect of this technique in the Civil War, including tactical deception, the provision of false orders, and the use of physiological warfare materials, as well as the direct exploitation of the transmitted information.[8]

President Abraham Lincoln was personally acquainted with the communications process and the associated use of codebooks and cipher disks.[9] Lincoln would leave his White House office and walk across to the War Department, where he used the privacy of the military telegraph office to think as well as to read and write messages to his commanders in the field. He often watched the encipherment and decipherment processes that were conducted by a few young civilians. He also benefited from the security and privacy of this office, which he used as he drafted other documents, including the Emancipation Proclamation.

Although the telegraph had already been used in military operations, the American Civil War saw its wide-scale use and raised awareness of the value of secure communications at the highest levels of government.

## July 1866

The first truly successful transatlantic cable was put into operation over essentially the same route used in 1858. It was laid by a single ship over a distance of about 1,700 nautical miles. Information could now be exchanged between continents in "near real time" as opposed to the fastest ship travel (approximately five days). The service was expensive (about $1 per character) and therefore did not attract general public use. Nevertheless, the first transatlantic cable was a major milestone in the growth of the telegraph industry.

The persistent efforts of the American businessman Cyrus Field were largely responsible for this success. A founder of the Atlantic Telegraph Company, he had been a primary sponsor of the 1858 effort. The U.S. Congress awarded him a special gold medal in 1867 in recognition of his work.[10]

## 1874

The French engineer Jean-Maurice-Emile Baudot received a patent for a telegraph code that used five-unit combinations of on and off signals of the same duration to represent the alphabet and selected machine functions. This code improved the mechanization of telegraphy. The Baudot code is called a five-bit binary code and can represent the twenty-six letters of the alphabet as well as numerals, punctuation marks, and the control of some machine functions (see appendix A for more information). Essentially, all early teletypes and teleprinters used some variant of this five-bit code. It remained in use for many years and is considered the ancestor of current similar codes that have grown to accommodate languages that do not use the Latin alphabet.

The telephone emerged and was quickly commercialized. The word *telephone* was derived from the Greek, meaning *far speaking*. Because telephones enabled individuals to speak to each other over distances in their native languages almost instantaneously, while preserving the many nuances of human speech, there was a great demand for this communications capability.

## March 1876

Alexander Graham Bell demonstrated the technology for the telephone.

Alexander Graham Bell (1847–1922). Now widely recognized as the inventor of the telephone, and quite possibly the best-known inventor in the world, Bell was born in Edinburgh, Scotland, and became a U.S. citizen in 1882. He was active and creative in many fields and had a lifetime interest in providing services to the deaf. *The Historical Society of Washington, DC, Kiplinger Library*

# May 1876

The International Telegraph Union was established at a meeting in Paris, France, by twenty member nations to provide a coordinating body for international standards and processes related to international communications.

# June 1876

Bell demonstrated his device at the Philadelphia Centennial. It enjoyed enthusiastic acceptance.

# July 1878

The Bell Telephone Company was officially formed.

# Early 1880s

The telephone was in wide commercial use (more than 60,000 units).

# 1884

By the mid-1880s, electromechanical aids were being applied to computing. John H. Patterson acquired the patents of James and John Ritty and established the National Cash Register Company.

Also in this year, Herman Hollerith applied for patents on the punch-card tabulating machine. Hollerith was the creator of a character code for encoding alphanumeric data on the punched cards. This card carried the well-known phrase, "Do Not Fold, Spindle, or Mutilate." This type of data coding and storage remained in use for more than eighty years and had wide application in the early computer industry. Hollerith also founded the Tabulating Machine Company.

In this same general time period, William S. Burroughs invented what he called an Adding and Listing Machine. This machine was the first to combine a calculator, a keyboard, and a printer into one operating unit. His products enjoyed widespread use.

# 1890

Hollerith's punch-card equipment was used in the U.S. Census, which meant that the data could be processed in about seven weeks as opposed to the previous time of more than two years.

Also about this time the German professor Gottlob Frege introduced his idea of predicate calculus, which eventually led to widespread use of algorithms to calculate and describe functions.

The general public accepted many of the new technological advances, governmental functions provided some of the applications, and a set of new businesses grew. As the new capabilities spread in all areas, they provoked even more new ideas. All three fields were primed for further progress.

Soon a new invention, the radio, would be added to the mix of technologies and would provoke further changes in the way business and governments operate.

# 4

# 1895–1939:
# THE INTRODUCTION
# OF RADIO STIMULATES
# NEW APPLICATIONS

The invention of the radio accelerated the process of separating communications from transportation.

The radio, known for many years as "the wireless," removed the limitations of wires. Of course, wires and cables remained in use to provide communications services and improvements as these technologies continued, but now radio provided new service options. Newer technologies seldom replace all of the earlier ones. Although old technologies tend to persist, it is the newer ones that open up new applications.

## 1895

The Italian inventor and businessman Guglielmo Marconi demonstrated radio technology over long ranges. This development showed obvious promise, and applications were quickly developed. Somewhat less obvious at first: long-range radio technology would require significant technical advancements in cryptography to ensure the privacy of its messages. However, concerns about access to a "wireless" transmission were present from the very early days. For example, Marconi applied for a British patent in 1896, and demonstrations of his invention were made in many locations. The instruments differed from those we recognize as "radio" today. The transmitter used a "spark-gap" apparatus associated with an induction coil, and the receiver used a device called a "coherer." At a demonstration to the American Institute of Electrical Engineers in New York in 1896, the first question from the floor was "Would any other induction coil produce the same effect as this one, or are these two instruments related so as to form a pair? If intelligence transmitted from one piece of apparatus could be read by any one of a hundred machines, this method of telegraphy would have its disadvantages."[1]

There were probably many motivations for this question, but one was undoubtedly the concern over the privacy and security of the messages sent via this new technology.

In retrospect it is clear that the invention of radio provoked the requirements for the next wave of improvements in cryptography.

### November 1899

The U.S. Navy conducted its first tests of ship-to-ship and ship-to-shore radio using the USS *New York*, USS *Massachusetts*, the USS *Porter*, and a shore station

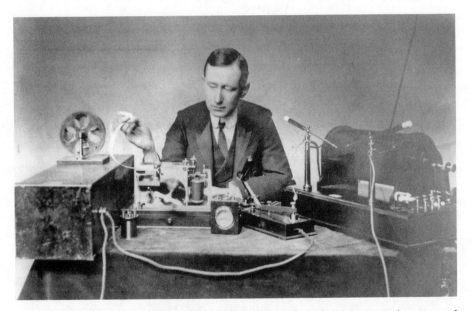

Guglielmo Marconi (1874–1937) poses in 1902 with some of the equipment that was used in his December 1901 demonstration of transatlantic communication between Poldhu, Cornwall, and St. John's, Newfoundland (now known as Signal Hill). The "key" for the transmitter is in the center. Marconi is holding the "inking" tape. Marconi was awarded a Nobel Prize in 1909 for his role in developing radio. *Science and Society Picture Library of the London Science Museum*

at the Highland Light at Navesink, New Jersey. The first "official" message was transmitted on November 2, 1899. The vast potential of radio for naval communications (both military and commercial) applications was now obvious.

## 1901

Marconi established a crude transatlantic radio communications capability.

## 1904

The U.S. Navy completed the installation of fifty-eight radio equipments on ships and shore stations, thereby launching their long-ranged communications system.

## 1906

Lee DeForest invented the vacuum tube triode, which would lead to practical electronic amplifiers.

## August 27, 1910

The first wireless message was transmitted from air to ground in a demonstration near Sheepshead Bay, New York. J. C. D. McCurdy was the pilot, and H. M. Horton designed the equipment.

## 1911

Charles Flint founded the Computing-Tabulating-Recording Co. (C-T-R), which manufactured and sold punch-card and tabulating equipment.

## World War I

The telegraph was joined by both the telephone and radio, making the security of communications increasingly important. The radio in particular exposed messages to many unintended recipients. However, no tools were available to integrate the encryption and communications processes. To send a secure message, one had to follow two separate processes—a manual encryption process and then transmission. This was cumbersome, slow, and often inaccurate. Nevertheless, encryption schemes grew increasingly complex and became the subject of study.

The military could not fully realize the impact of radio communications on command-and-control processes until it could secure messages more easily and on a more widespread basis. Despite their limitations, all parties in the war used telegraphy, as well as the radio and telephone. The need to exploit signals was not limited to diplomatic messages, although the famous Zimmerman telegram is an outstanding example of the importance of cryptanalysis in diplomatic communications.[2]

This complex story involves the instructions sent by the German foreign minister, Arthur Zimmerman, to his ambassador to the United States. The encrypted telegraph cable was intercepted and deciphered by the British. The contents clearly indicated that the Germans were planning not only unrestricted submarine warfare, but also an alliance with Mexico that would lead to the "return" of territory to Mexico from the United States. The situation was made clear to President Woodrow Wilson, and the contents of the message were actually released in the American press. America soon entered the war. There were many factors involved, including hostile German submarine activities, but there is no doubt that the Zimmerman telegram played an important role in convincing Wilson to support the entry of the United States into the World War I. Historian David Kahn describes the work surrounding the Zimmerman telegram as follows: "No other single cryptanalysis has had such enormous consequences. Never before or since has so much turned upon the solution of a secret message. For those few moments in time, the codebreakers held history in the palm of their hand."[3]

U.S. Army direction-finding equipment, 1918. This mobile radio direction-finding truck (or "tractor") is shown as it was deployed in France to support tactical field operations. The operator physically rotated the rooftop antenna to determine the strongest reception and then, sometime in concert with another similar system, could get a rough "fix" on the location of the transmitting equipment. Crude, but still worthwhile. The government used similar equipment along the Mexican border before World War I. *Center for Cryptologic History*

And to think, those talented codebreakers were still mainly using paper and pencil! Of course, vacuum-tube devices were in use, and some were deployed in tactical situations.

## January 25, 1915

The first transcontinental telephone call, New York to San Francisco, was completed via land lines.

This call provided a dramatic punctuation mark in the separation of communications and transportation. American Telephone and Telegraph Co. (AT&T) conducted this call with the inventor of the telephone, Alexander Graham Bell, located in New York, and his longtime assistant, Thomas Watson, participating in San Francisco. During the course of their conversation Bell repeated his 1876 first-ever voice message to Watson when he said, "Mr. Watson, come here, I want to see you." This time Watson replied, "Mr. Bell, I will, but it would take me a week now!"

The separation from transportation was now complete for most practical purposes as communicators now had a viable choice for sending messages.

## 1915

At this time, experiments were conducted on the transmission of voice by radio across the Atlantic Ocean.

This general timeframe also saw an increasing realization that while a missing physically transmitted message might at one time have raised suspicions that it may have fallen into unintended hands, now there might be no such built-in warning. This realization provided motivation for improving the security of communications and shifted attention to cryptologic activities.

## 1915–20s

Capt. Parker Hitt of the U.S. Army wrote *Manual for the Solution of Military Ciphers*, which was a practical aid to cryptanalysts and the first American book on the subject. In 1917, he created a device consisting of multiple strips of mixed alphabets that could be placed in a holder and, when moved relative to each other, were used to create ciphertext. This scheme was made into a multidisk cylinder version in 1922 and became known as the M-94. Thomas Jefferson and Robert Patterson would have recognized it immediately, although Captain Hitt had no knowledge of their work. The sliding-strips version took on the military nomenclature of M-138-A. Both versions were used in World War II (see photo on page 40).

The M-94 cipher device. Shown here in a photo from an old technical paper, the M-94 was both rugged and simple in concept. Field-usable devices must be rugged and easy to use in all types of environments. Although it is an "off-line" device that only performs an encryption or decryption function, it was a proven performer for many years. Depending on the skills of the cryptanalyst and the exact techniques involved in its use, it could provide temporary message security by means of the time delay it caused the enemy cryptanalysts. *Center for Cryptologic History*

# 1917

During World War II, electromechanical tools were introduced into cryptologic activities. The American inventor Edward Hebern produced the first encipherment system using wired rotors.[4] In such a system, an electrical path is created through multiple rotors that are electrically connected to each other through contacts; each has unique internal wiring. The output of the electrical path is

The M-138-A in use. A desk-based analyst of the World War II era uses the sliding strips of the M-138-A (above her left hand) and reference material to encode a message for later transmission.

therefore changed for each sequential input of letters or symbols depending on the "stepping" of the various rotors relative to each other.

Hebern was committed to creating a business in cryptography and was interested in both industrial and governmental customers. He entered into a contractual relationship with the government and did sell some equipment. However, the government contracts were a disaster and his business failed. Long legal battles followed until 1958. He never gained true compensation for his efforts or even recognition for his inventive contributions to cryptography. This was a poor chapter in government-industry relationships.

1917 also produced a major breakthrough in the mechanization of cryptography. An AT&T engineer, Gilbert Vernam, imagined a way to use the five-character Baudot code (used in telegraphy to represent all letters and symbols of a message) as an integral part of an automatic encryption process. At that time, punched paper tape was the input medium for the teletypewriters. Vernam proposed the creation of a separate punched tape containing the cryptographic key

A Hebern wired-rotor machine. Edward Hebern founded the first company in the United States that was based on providing encipherment equipment. He owned many patents in the field, but the most important of his inventions was the wired-rotor concept that was used in many later devices. The excellent craftsmanship of his machine shop is apparent in this unit, which is on display at the National Cryptologic Museum.

characters. The two tapes would be "summed" electrically by a set of contacts and relays according to a rather simple set of logical rules to create ciphertext. The ciphertext could be transmitted as the message text was read into the machine. The system was symmetrical: the receiving system needed to have the same key and was required to keep it in synchronism with the ciphertext, but that was not difficult to do. What was new was that for the first time, messages could be enciphered, transmitted, received, and deciphered in an automatic process. Although this system had many obvious advantages, it was not put into widespread use until the U.S. Army finally adopted it just prior to World War II.

## 1918

While on active duty with the U.S. Army Signal Corps in Paris, Edwin Armstrong invented the super heterodyne receiver, which improved the sensitivity and selectivity of receivers greatly. After the war, Armstrong would return to Columbia University and continue to make major contributions to the development of radio.

Also in this year, Howard Krum was awarded a patent on a device that solved one of the major problems in telegraphy, the difficulties in keeping the sending and receiving units in synchronism. Implementing of this "start-stop" method of sending the Baudot and other codes permitted the direct transmission of type-writer key-strokes to a receiving printer. Commercial applications, particularly in the newspaper and financial businesses, spread quickly in the 1920s. A variety of new companies were established for the purpose of producing teleprinter equipment and operating the communications systems.

## 1919

Hugo Koch of the Netherlands filed a patent for a rotor-based encryption system, which he intended for industrial use.

## November 1920

The station with the first commercial broadcast license, KDKA, Pittsburgh, Pennsylvania, popularized broadcast radio with news of the presidential election returns.

## 1922

The first commercial regularly scheduled broadcasting stations in the United States began operations (WWJ, Detroit, Michigan, and WLW, Cincinnati, Ohio). Radios became increasingly commonplace in the home.

Television, distant seeing, added the active visual dimension to the communications process. Major technical innovations continued at a rapid pace in all of the related technologies and the communications industries, which were expanding to both new customers and new services.

Philo T. Farnsworth developed the first image-scanning system. A prolific inventor, he continued his work in the television field and, with the support of private investors, demonstrated the first electronic television in 1927.

## 1923

Vladimir Zworykin, born and educated in Russia, emigrated to the United States in 1919. After working for Westinghouse, he developed and patented the iconoscope and kinescope, essential ingredients for an all-electronic television. The basic techniques made possible creating images from live situations and simultaneously displaying them.

# 1924

Thomas Watson, president of C-T-R, changed its name to International Business Machines (IBM) Corporation.

# 1926

The first demonstration of television technology in England took place.

# 1927

Commercial transatlantic radio-telephone service was inaugurated between the United States and England by AT&T.

Also in 1927 Hugo Koch assigned his rights to his 1919 patent to the German businessman-engineer Arthur Scherbius. Scherbius soon created the now-famous ENIGMA machine, which was to become a major cryptographic tool of the World War II era. Once the machine was adopted by the German armed forces, many variants came into existence.

All of the ENIGMA machines were "off-line" tools; that is, the messages had to be both written and transmitted by processes separate from their encryption. These machines created enormous challenges for Allied cryptanalysts.[5]

# 1928

Although it was originally intended for aircraft use as a radio compass, the French engineer Henri Busignies offered his patent for a direct-indicating radio direction finder to the French subsidiary of ITT Corp.

The Federal Communications Commission (FCC) was established.

# 1929

Zworykin demonstrated an all-electronic television system to a convention of radio engineers. This led him to a long-term affiliation with the Radio Corporation of America (RCA). Although it would take many more years of development and many legal battles between RCA and Farnsworth and his backers before television became commonly used, the basic engineering building-blocks were now in place.

# 1930

Vannevar Bush of the Massachusetts Institute of Technology (MIT) developed a "differential analyzer," which was a large analog computer primarily intended for solving differential equations.

An ENIGMA machine in its field-carrying case. ENIGMAs were made in many versions. This one has three rotors, which are visible at the top of the control panel. The plugboard at the front of the unit was also a part of the elaborate crypto-key system. These reliable and sturdy units provided good security when used properly. *Center for Cryptologic History*

# 1931

Radio-telephone service started between the U.S. mainland and Hawaii.

# 1934

Radio-telephone service started between the U.S. mainland and Japan (Tokyo). The International Telegraph Union changed its name to the International Telecommunication Union to more completely reflect the scope of modern communications techniques.

# 1935

The American cryptologist Frank Rowlett invented a fundamental improvement to the wired-rotor machine.[6] Rowlett worked with William Friedman on the idea, and they developed a way to incorporate a second set of wired rotors into the design of the current U.S. Army five-rotor machine called the M-134-T2.[7] The function of this rotor set was to drive the relative positioning of the cipher-rotors in a quasi-random manner. This had the potential for providing great improvements in the cryptographic security of the system.

The Army did not immediately adopt the improved system, but the U.S. Navy, under the guidance of Laurance F. Safford, did pick up on the idea in 1937.

In 1938, the Navy entered into a contract with the Teletype Corporation to produce the new system, which was called the Mark II ECM (the Mark I was a derivative of an earlier Hebern machine). Although the services did not share technical information in any routine manner (to say the least), an early production model of the Mark II ECM was demonstrated to the Army Signal Corps and the Signal Intelligence Service early in 1940. All agreed that the machine was the best available for high-level ciphers. Both the Army and the Navy adopted the machine, which used ten rotors for the cipher operations and five rotors for control of the stepping. A special third set of control rotors was developed to permit joint Army-Navy communications. The Army used the designator SIGABA and the Navy added the designator CSP888, but it was also called ECM for short. For the first time, the Army and Navy could communicate securely using the same machine. Eventually the Teletype Corp. would produce about ten thousand of these devices, which permitted the United States to enter World War II with the tools for a defensive information advantage. Postwar analysis revealed that it was a powerful advantage; the SIGABA/ECM machines were never exploited.

Frank Rowlett (1908–1998). A graduate of Emory and Henry College, Mr. Rowlett was hired by William Friedman and joined the Army Signal Intelligence Service (SIS) in 1930. He was a major contributor to many World War II cryptanalytic and cryptographic successes and remained active in the field for many years. The building that houses the National Security Agency's Information Assurance Directorate is named in his honor. *Center for Cryptologic History*

William Friedman (1891–1969). William Friedman was born in imperial Russia and emigrated to the United States in 1893. A graduate of Cornell University, he soon became interested in cryptology and served as a cryptologic officer in World War I. He led the technical efforts of the U.S. Army's Signal Intelligence Service during World War II and was responsible for recruiting and training many of that era's most successful cryptologists. He also made many original technical contributions to the field. His wife, Elizebeth S. Friedman, was a skilled cryptographer in her own right. Among other things, she worked for the U.S. Department of Treasury in the 1920s and succeeded in providing information that was essential in gaining convictions for many criminals through her cryptanalytic efforts. NSA's original operations building in Ft. Meade, Maryland, is now named the William and Elizebeth Friedman Building. *Center for Cryptologic History*

Laurance F. Safford (1890–1973). A 1916 graduate of the United States Naval Academy, he was appointed in 1924 to command the "research desk" of the Code and Signal Section within the Office of Naval Communications. From this position he led the development of naval cryptologic activities and organized the worldwide naval collection and direction-finding effort that was one of the keys to the success in World War II. He also attracted other experts to this field, including Agnes Meyer Driscoll, Joseph Rochefort, and Joseph Wenger. The total team eventually succeeded in breaking the Japanese naval codes. Also, his collaboration with the Army and his direct contributions to the development and deployment of SIGABA were unique efforts that strengthened American cryptologic capability at a crucial time in history. *Center for Cryptologic History*

SIGABA. In this view, the complex rotors that controlled the random stepping are visible on the top of the machine. It is also clear that in this model, the output of the encryption process was a printed tape that eliminated many possibilities of error in the total transmission process. *Center for Cryptologic History*

## 1936

Alan Turing of Cambridge University wrote *On Computable Numbers*,[8] which was a mathematical proof that it was possible to build a computer that was not restricted to solving only one problem or class of problems. This work also provided the theoretical basis for modern software.

Alan Turing (1912–1954). Elected a fellow of King's College, Cambridge, in 1935, he soon published his work that demonstrated the possibility of using a machine that followed rules to perform what we now routinely call computation. He joined the cryptologic work of the Government Code and Cypher School at Bletchley Park full-time in 1939 and made major contributions to many important intelligence problems. *Library of King's College, Cambridge University*

## 1937–38

Claude Shannon of MIT and George Stibitz of BTL demonstrated that Boolean algebra could be implemented electrically. In Germany, Konrad Zuse applied some of his earlier work and completed two electromechanical binary computers, the Z1 and Z2, which used memory.

## 1939

A major public demonstration of RCA's television took place at the World's Fair in New York. At this same event BTL demonstrated the voice synthesizer which, among other things, provided one of building blocks of SIGSALY, digital secure voice communications in World War II.

Computation with electronic circuits arrived this same year when John J. Atanasoff and Clifford Berry at Iowa State College produced a prototype electronic computer using binary arithmetic. Little evidence remains of any significant application of this work, but in 1973 a complex court decision identified it as the first automatic digital computer. Although this point is still argued, there is little debate that it was a significant step forward.

World War II would bring immediate national attention and increased resources to the developments in all three fields.

# 5

# MID-1930s–1950:
# WORLD WAR II
# ACCELERATES DEVELOPMENTS
# IN ALL FIELDS

The tools of the cryptologic arts and sciences draw from, and sometimes provoke, leading-edge developments in communications and computer engineering.

Wartime makes powerful nations aware that they cannot afford second-place status in any important area of technology. The World War II era brought technological advancements in many diverse areas, including landing craft, atomic energy, radar, jet propulsion, ballistic missiles, medicine, and mass production techniques. Technology advances in our three areas—cryptology, communications, and computers—are more closely related than was generally apparent before the 1970s, when some wartime systems information was declassified. We begin this chapter with wartime cryptologic activities, building on some of the examples that we presented in chapter 1. These activities are intertwined and do not lend themselves to a strict timeline presentation, but we have organized their timespans in a general chronological sequence and have included some dates for the sake of clarity.

In the mid-1930s the Japanese, in great secrecy, were developing their own encipherment machine using a different electromechanical device than that of the German ENIGMA. The Japanese employed the stepping switch that had been developed for worldwide telephone use. Use of the stepping switch offered an entirely different technique for creating the varying electrical paths required for the encipherment process. The most famous of the machines that resulted from this particular design approach was the Angooki Taipu B or Hinoki cipher machine. It came to be called PURPLE by the American cryptographers. To this day, no non-Japanese person has probably ever seen either a PURPLE machine or an original description of its design. Nevertheless, American cryptographers led by Frank Rowlett, and supported by the Army engineer Lt. Col. Leo Rosen and the cryptographer Genevieve Grotjan (among others), developed a method of deciphering the machine, even though they only had ciphertext to work with! By late 1940, the American cryptographers were able to read messages from the PURPLE machines. The Allies' ability to exploit this breakthrough only improved throughout the war; they eventually shared the information with the British. This sharing of information between the United States and Britain led to what remains a unique international agreement in the history of cryptology.

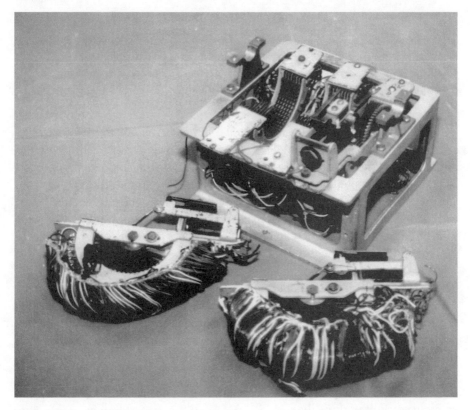

Remains of a PURPLE crypto machine. This photograph shows the telephone-based switching technology that the Japanese used in their cryptographic machines. The disciplined destruction of their equipment after the war was typical of their attention to detail in cryptologic activities. *Center for Cryptologic History*

The Japanese JADE cryptographic machine. This close technical relative of the PURPLE machine was designed for use at sea rather than for office use in diplomatic locations. It could also be used in shore installations. This unit was captured on Saipan during the latter part of World War II. *Center for Cryptologic History*

The design of the PURPLE machine has a theoretical cryptographic security greater than that of ENIGMA. The people who broke this machine accomplished one of the most amazing feats of cryptanalysis the world has ever seen.[1] The Japanese completely destroyed their cryptographic equipment after the war. The largest piece of a PURPLE machine ever seen by Americans was recovered in 1945 from the basement of the Japanese embassy in Berlin. It is safe to assume that PURPLE used the same engineering techniques as JADE, another Japanese system captured after the war.

A cryptanalyst's tools in late 1930 to mid-1940 were also electromechanical. The most basic and widespread devices were commercial IBM card-sorting machines and their associated input-output devices such as keyboards, tabulators, electric typewriters, and key-punch equipment. Literally millions of punched cards were used by cryptanalysts. Sometimes special modifications were made in the IBM machines to allow for new operations, but most of the uses paralleled the original design expectations of the equipment. The availability of this type of equipment and the support of the related industries was a huge help to the total cryptologic effort of the Allies.

Other special-purpose cryptanalytic equipment was also electromechanical in nature. The BOMBE,[2] which was used to recover key settings of the ENIGMA machine, was an engineering marvel. Eventually produced in many variants in

Data preparation at Arlington Hall Station, Virginia, circa 1943. A production line for preparing and checking the inputs for further cryptanalysis is conducted by a team led by the Women's Army Corps (WACs). This important task was aided by specialized equipment that produced a common format nonmagnetic tape output for use in the cryptanalytic process. *U.S. Army*

both England and the United States, the basic functional design of the BOMBE was a product of the cryptologic activities at Bletchley Park; however, the engineering required to implement the desired functions and to produce operating systems was a task that was shared between government personnel and engineers at the National Cash Register (NCR) Company in Dayton, Ohio. The NCR team was led by Joseph R. Desch. This very talented team worked under conditions of strict security and did a masterful job of selecting technologies that could be applied within the limited time available. The design and manufacturing process was successfully accomplished under severe schedule pressure and involved both civilians and more than six hundred Women Appointed for Voluntary Emergency Services (WAVES) who were integrated into the Dayton operation. Joseph Desch received the Congressional Medal for Merit in 1947 for his contributions to this program.[3]

An impressive installation of this machine was at the Naval Communications Annex, where more than a hundred units were used. It was a noisy, busy workplace

A WAVE adjusts the operation of a BOMBE, circa 1945. This photograph was taken on the second deck of building four of the Navy's complex on Nebraska Avenue in Washington, DC. The BOMBEs were amazing electromechanical devices that could make data comparisons several orders of magnitude faster than the German cryptographers had imagined. Although the individual parts of the system were available on the marketplace of the day, the innovative system application of the components resulted in unprecedented accomplishments. *Center for Cryptologic History*

BOMBE operations on the second deck of the Naval Communications Annex, May 1945. Each BOMBE weighed about five thousand pounds and there were fifty on each of two floors. The installation required special power and air conditioning. *Center for Cryptologic History*

that was staffed primarily by WAVES and operated twenty-four hours a day, seven days a week. The workers who operated the BOMBEs faced a complex and demanding process. A glimpse of the complexity is given in this description:

> Operationally, menus for setting up a BOMBE were typed by WAVES in the cryptanalytic section and were forwarded to a BOMBE supervisor by pneumatic tube. The supervisor then gave the menu to a BOMBE operator. The menu consisted of instructions to set up the BOMBE wheels, how to place the rotors, and whether a short or long run was desired. The short run took ten or fifteen minutes. After setting up, the BOMBE was turned on and it would run until a "hit" occurred. A "hit" indicated that an electrical pathway had been found. The BOMBE was running too fast to mechanically record a "hit," so this was done by an electronic memory circuit. When the machine recorded a "hit," a brake was automatically applied to stop the drive shaft. A clutch and rewind motor were then engaged to reverse direction until the drive shaft was stopped on the correct "hit" position as directed by the memory circuit. . . . .

The resultant "hit" information was recorded by a printer showing the correct rotor positions. The WAVE operators would pass this information through a small door to another supervisor's room. The recovered keys on the printout were sent back to the cryptanalytic unit by the BOMBE supervisor by pneumatic tube. After the key recovery was confirmed by a cryptanalyst, a WAVE typed out the German U-boat intercepted messages on ENIGMA machine analogues, which then produced German plain text.[4]

By itself, technology cannot solve such complex problems. Talented, imaginative, and dedicated people are required at every stage of the process. The whole World War II story of cryptography is testament to this fact.

The cryptanalytic machine used to decipher the PURPLE traffic was a deceptively simple-looking system that, like the PURPLE machine itself, was based on telephone-switching units.

Operation of a PURPLE analog machine, circa 1943. The WAC operator on the left is performing the setup of the deciphering machine while the input and output are controlled by the operator on the right who is using modified electric typewriters. The office-like environment here contrasts to the BOMBE operations elsewhere and was enabled by the basic technical nature of the encryption-decryption process. *Center for Cryptologic History*

Though speculative, it is thought that the sole remaining artifact of the PUR-PLE machine may have been used to encrypt some of the most important Japanese messages of World War II—namely, the reports of the Japanese ambassador to Germany, Gen. Oshima Hiroshi. For example, in early November 1943 he sent a detailed message to Tokyo describing the fortifications and military order of battle for the Normandy area. It was intercepted and decrypted by the Army Signal Security Service. Obviously, his description was extremely helpful to the Allies in their planning for D-Day in Europe. Both President Roosevelt and Prime Minister Churchill would soon read these and other similar messages. Because of the efforts of the American cryptanalysts, General Oshima had, in effect, been an unwitting spy for the Allies during his time in Berlin.[5]

Although they were slow and often not completely integrated into the communications systems, the electromechanical cryptographic equipment of both the Axis and the Allied forces did enable military command-and-control systems to use radio efficiently, even when the forces were engaged over entire hemispheres. Diplomatic use of radio also depended on this technology. The superiority of the Allies' equipment for both encryption and cryptanalysis was extremely important in the war effort, a fact clearly appreciated by both President Roosevelt and Prime Minister Churchill.

The large-scale application of vacuum-tube electronics continued to support a wide variety of new capabilities and the industrial strength to sustain growth.

## January 1940

At his own expense, Edwin Armstrong obtained a Federal Communications Commission (FCC) permit for the first frequency modulation (FM) radio broadcast station. This station demonstrated the practicality of his invention of the modulation technique. However, expansion of the FM broadcasting industry was delayed by many legal, business, and bureaucratic battles.

## 1941

The Naval Research Laboratory (NRL) evaluated shipboard versions of the Busignies-designed ITT radio direction finder. The positive evaluation led the U.S. Navy to deploy this type of equipment to all escort vessels.

## Late 1930s to Early 1940s

Just before the outbreak of World War II, neither the United States nor the United Kingdom had a truly secure method of communicating by voice. The groundwork for a solution to this important problem was available at Bell Telephone

Laboratories (BTL). Based partly on a voice synthesizer, which simulated speech by electronically assembling the basic elements of voice waveforms, and which was demonstrated at the 1939 World's Fair, BTL produced a prototype voice security system and demonstrated it to the U.S. Army. An initial contract was awarded in 1942 for two systems. Official operation of the system began in mid-1943. By the end of the war, more than ten systems had been deployed and were successfully used for high-level secret conversations related to the conduct of the war and the delicate diplomatic negotiations that followed. The system was called SIGSALY.[6]

SIGSALY terminals were large and power-hungry, but provided a reasonably reliable solution to a complex problem. Hundreds of vacuum tubes were used in the system. For example, there were 384 thyratron tubes alone in each terminal (thyratrons were gas-filled tubes and were used as switches in the logic circuits). The digital keying system involved a complex use of advanced disc-recording equipment and a crucial physical key-distribution support operation. The tech-

A SIGSALY installation. Each installation was unique, but this photograph conveys the complexity and size of the system. The phonograph turntables that reproduced the cryptographic key are on the right of the picture. An associated HF radio receiver was a major tool in the process of ensuring that the local system time standard matched the international time signals. The approximate weight of the forty racks of equipment and other materials in a terminal was fifty-five tons! *Center for Cryptologic History*

nology of the day required many innovations and inventions. The system was not an improvement of any existing system; it was a unique design. The BTL team invented not only the first truly digital voice-communication system, but also the means to encrypt the voice, the means to transmit it, and the means to train the operators of the system. This system, shown in one deployment, can legitimately be called the beginning of the digital communications age.

# 1943

SIGSALY system is put into official operation in June. For the first time people can communicate securely by voice over long distances. Terminals were eventually established in Washington, DC, London, Paris, North Africa, Hawaii, Guam, Manila, and Australia, among other places. Each terminal had installation challenges. Systems were also deployed after the war to other locations, including Berlin, Frankfurt, and Tokyo.

In London, the bulk of the SIGSALY equipment was housed in the basement of an annex to Selfridge's department store while the instrument used by Churchill and his staff was about a mile away in the War Rooms under the Admiralty Building and near the prime minister's residence at 10 Downing Street. The Washington, DC, end of the system was installed in the recently completed Pentagon in the summer of 1943. The original installation schedule planned for White House location, but the Pentagon in Virginia was chosen to allow senior members of the military easier access to the system (and possibly to give President Roosevelt better control over his own schedule so he would not be interrupted at all hours by callers).

Much of the engineering work was kept secret until 1976, and although the inventors were eventually recognized for their patented work, the true impact of this system's accomplishments went unrecognized until more than thirty years after its initial deployment.

Also in 1943 BTL completes its development model of the AN/TRC-6, the world's first mobile multichannel microwave relay system, and delivers it to the Signal Corps. This system offered eight independent channels of communication by means of one radio transmitter and receiving system. The system provided the channels by using variable times between the transmission of pulses (called a time-division multiplex, pulse-position modulation system). They operated in "line-of-sight" modes in the 5 GHz frequency range with parabolic dish antenna systems. Because of the narrow beamwidth (approximately 2 degrees) of the transmission between the relay towers, this system was difficult to intercept. By the end of the war, eighty-five classified systems were deployed. The AN/TRC-6 was the forerunner of today's multichannel, high-capacity, microwave radio systems.

Setting the key wheel pins on the M-209-B. This photo from an Army training manual shows the compact and rugged construction of this widely used off-line cipher machine. The entire unit, including a canvas carrying case, weighed about seven pounds. *U.S. Army*

Advanced technology does not always immediately replace reliable and useful techniques that have operational advantages. Vacuum-tube electronics could not supplant all other types of encipherment tools. A good example of this fact is the all-mechanical U.S. Army M-209 that was placed into wide operational service starting in 1942. This compact, six-pound, completely manual machine generates a polyalphabetic cipher that provided reasonable security for tactical use. The efficient and practical design was brought to the United States by Boris Hagelin, who operated a Swedish company engaged in producing cryptographic equipment. The Hagelin family escaped through Italy in 1940 and soon brought the design to the U.S. Army for testing. After some negotiations and tests, the Army accepted the device and awarded a contract to L. C. Smith & Corona Typewriters, Inc., to begin production. Before the war was over, they had produced more than 140,000 units. Hagelin had better luck than Hebern with his government contracts and became a millionaire from the royalties.[7]

Setting the machine in operation was manageable in tactical circumstances, and field use of the machine was relatively easy. Both of these characteristics remain absolutely essential for use of cryptographic tools in tactical environments. The M-209 was the best of its kind.

Although SIGSALY was a technological marvel for its time, the requirements for secure voice communications in the field far outstripped the ability of the technologists of the day. High-level military and political leaders needed to maintain the privacy of their conversations with each other, as did units in the field. SIGSALY-like machines were simply too large and too complex to meet the tactical requirements. In the face of this challenge, Native American "codetalkers" provided an essential capability for tactical voice communications. The basic idea for using rare languages for voice security can be traced at least back to World War I, when Native American codetalkers were used in combat by the Army's 142nd Infantry Regiment, 36th Infantry Division, in the Argonne Forest battles of 1918. In this case, eight members of the Choctaw tribe provided voice security. During World War II the Choctaws, Comanches, Winnebagos, Pawnees, Kiowas, Cherokees, Navajos, and possibly others played the same role in the Army. Specialized codebooks were still required because these native languages lacked vocabulary for some military equipment and tactics.

The U.S. Marine Corps used Navajos exclusively; more than four hundred served in this program during the war. Both Army and Marine Corps programs were so successful that soon the number of Native Americans who could speak both English and their native language was insufficient to meet the demand. Language schools were started by the Army, but the war ended before graduates could be deployed.

The codetalkers served bravely and capably, contributing their unique skills to the protection of the tactical voice communications in many dangerous situations. It would be many years before advances in technology would permit mere tools to take their place.

Vacuum-tube electronics also provided the mechanism to create the most technically advanced cryptanalytic system of the time. This system, COLOSSUS, was the world's first large electronic digital computer.[8] The driving force for the invention was the German Lorenz SZ42 encipherment machine, which presented a complex problem to the British. Although the cryptanalysts had not seen an actual Lorenz machine, they had been able to break the cipher by laborious manual work. The importance of the decrypted text demanded a much more powerful and faster method of attack.

Dr. Tommy Flowers (1905–1998), circa 1996. Dr. Flowers was the creative engineer who was responsible for the detail design and implementation of the COLOSSUS system at Bletchley Park. His ideas and design capability were essential elements in the revolutionary accomplishment. After the war he returned to his work at the British Post Office and his wartime accomplishments were not made public until the 1970s. *Anthony Sale*

A view of the COLOSSUS system, circa 1944. This view of the installation at Bletchley Park shows the physical design of the system. The equipment on the right of the photograph is the mechanical part of the electro-optical data-input system. *Anthony Sale*

COLOSSUS provided the tools to mount that attack. Based on the analytic needs of the cryptanalysts, which were provided by mathematician Max Newman, a young engineer at the British Post Office, Dr. Tommy Flowers, set out to design and develop the computer. With his talented team, he produced the first unit in about seven months and it was ready for operation at the end of 1943.

The input to COLOSSUS was delivered by special electro-optical devices that read Baudot code from punched paper tape at a rate of five thousand characters per second. These devices were also a technical advancement that was led by Dr. Arnold Lynch.

More than 1,500 vacuum tubes were used in a COLOSSUS, but they proved to be reasonably reliable. The parallel aspects of the design permitted it to perform a Boolean operation about every two microseconds on each of five input channels. This still-remarkable performance was unimaginable at the time to all but the inventors of the system.

Another view of COLOSSUS, circa 1944. This picture was taken about the same time as the first and illustrates more detail of the physical design of the original system. Dr. Flowers's experience with the design of telephone switching systems is evident. *Anthony Sale*

COLOSSUS was very successful; ten versions were in operation by the end of the war. Secrecy concerns drove actions that eventually resulted in the destruction of all of the machines along with most of the documentation. The entire system remained a secret until the 1970s, when this remarkable accomplishment began to be given its rightful place in history. One unit has been reconstructed under the leadership of Anthony Sale and was put into operation at the Bletchley Park Museum in 1996.

In the early to mid-1940s there were also very creative cryptanalytic systems that were combinations of electromechanical tools and vacuum-tube electronic circuitry. One of these was called Superscritcher.[9] This was a digital switching unit that used more than a thousand vacuum tubes. The purpose of the unit was to speed up some of the logic functions of the ENIGMA analysis by a factor of at least one hundred. This successful project was conducted by personnel of the U.S. Army Signal Security Agency under the leadership of Lt. Col. Leo Rosen and 1st Lt. Donald MacRae.

Electronic computer activities also proceed at a fast pace in the United States. In 1943, under the creative direction of John Mauchly and J. Presper Eckert, work starts at the Moore School of Electrical Engineering of the University of Pennsylvania on the Electronic Numerical Integrator and Computer (ENIAC). This work was intended to support ballistics studies done at the Aberdeen Proving Ground of the U.S. Army. The entire design team (they knew nothing of the work on COLOS-SUS) made many basic contributions to the art, science, and business of computing.[10]

An early proponent of this work was Army Lt. Herman Goldstine, who held a Ph.D. in mathematics and had worked at the university prior to joining the Army. Lieutenant Goldstine's technically talented wife, Adele Goldstine, was directly involved in the project, training programmers and authoring a variety of technical publications related to ENIAC.

## 1945

John von Neumann, who was with the Institute for Advanced Studies (IAS) at Princeton and was aware of the work of Mauchly and Eckert, wrote a report entitled *First Draft of a Report on the EDVAC* (Electronic Discrete Variable Computer), which contained a vision of essentially all the computing functions that would be used for the next forty years of computing development. This report, though never formally published, was eagerly sought by most people involved in the field. Dr. von Neumann is credited with many innovations, including the stored program, although the origin of many of these ideas is still the matter of some debate.

Dr. von Neumann (1903–1957) was born in Budapest, Hungary, and completed his doctoral degree in 1926 at the University of Budapest. He visited Princeton University in 1930, and three years later was appointed to the original staff of IAS. He retained that position for the remainder of his life. He became a U.S. citizen and participated in scientific work supporting World War II. His work in computer architecture was extremely important. The IAS computer was completed in the late 1940s and served as a prototype for computer designers for many years.

On a lighter note, 1945 was also the year when computer pioneer Grace Hopper found the first computer "bug"—a moth trapped in the contacts of a relay that brought work to a halt on the experimental Mark II at Harvard University. In the mid-1980s, after a long career in computer science and related fields, she became a rear admiral in the U.S. Navy.[11]

## 1946

ENIAC, started in 1943 and the United States' first full-scale electronic digital computer, was completed and tested at the Moore School of Electrical Engineering at the University of Pennsylvania.

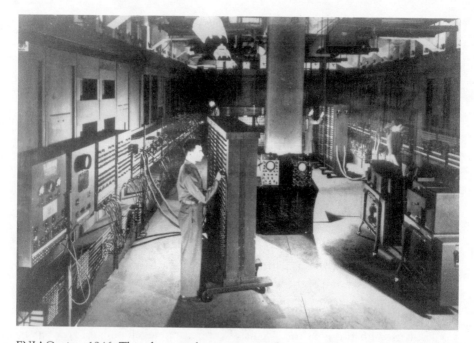

ENIAC, circa 1946. This photograph gives some indication of the size and extent of the ENIAC system. It was a programmable machine using more than seventeen thousand vacuum tubes and requiring more than 170 kilowatts of power to operate. It occupied almost two thousand square feet of laboratory space. Although never used for its wartime purpose, it did perform on a wide variety of problems and remained in operation until 1955. *Rare Book and Manuscript Library, Van Pelt–Dietrich Library Center, University of Pennsylvania*

In this same year, the Moore School of Electrical Engineering conducted a series of public workshops on computers that included many researchers in the field. It was well attended by representatives of industry, government, and academia. This event had a great influence on the development of the industry.

After his wartime service ended, Dr. Goldstine joined Dr. von Neumann at Princeton University and in 1958 joined IBM as director of research.

Postwar business ventures in electronic computers and communications got off to a fast start. In 1946, a key year for business reasons, two important new companies were founded. One, the Eckert-Mauchly Computer Corporation (EMCC), was the outgrowth of the founders' work at the University of Pennsylvania on ENIAC under contract to the U.S. Army Ordinance Department. The other, Engineering

Research Associates (ERA), was founded by William Norris, who had been a member of the U.S. Navy's cryptanalytic organization in World War II.[12] ERA's primary customer was the Navy's cryptographic element and, subsequently, the organization that became incorporated into the National Security Agency in 1952.

Also in 1946, the first public mobile telephone service is introduced in twenty-five American cities. Although it is not connected to the general switched networks, the public demand exceeds its capability.

The invention of the transistor would soon enable many advanced applications and further developments in many fields.

## 1947

The transistor was invented at BTL. John Bardeen, William Shockley, and Walter Brattain would share the Nobel Prize in 1956 for this revolutionary invention.

Because the transistor is based on the principles of solid-state physics and could perform signal amplification and switching function entirely differently than the existing vacuum-tube circuitry, the term "solid-state electronics" soon came into wide use.

## 1948

The first magnetic drum memory suitable for use in digital computers was put into service by ERA. This system, DEMON, was created for use by Navy cryptographers.

While at BTL, Claude E. Shannon published A Mathematical Theory of Communications.[13] The ideas in this important paper had a direct impact on many aspects of future communications systems. The paper also seemed to have contained the first published use of the word bit in an information context.

That same year, Richard Hamming, also at BTL, developed a coding technique that could find and correct errors in blocks of data. This work, combined with that of Shannon, prompted developments that were soon applied in both computing and communications systems.

## 1949

The Massachusetts Institute of Technology placed Whirlwind into operation. This was the first computer intended for real-time applications.

## 1949–50

FCC hearings found the Columbia Broadcasting System (CBS) of television transmission sufficiently advanced to permit general use. However, production was cur-

Claude E. Shannon (1916–2001). Dr. Shannon made important and fundamental contributions to all three fields of communication, computers, and cryptology. He is considered to be the father of modern information theory. *Lucent Technologies Inc./Bell Labs*

tailed in the interest of national defense, seemingly owing to continuing problems in Asia (including the Korean conflict), but they were put aside relatively quickly.

Postwar activities had now transferred important new technologies into the public sector, and the stage was set for additional dramatic advances.

# 6

# 1950–1969:
# THE INTRODUCTION OF
# SOLID-STATE ELECTRONICS AND
# SATELLITE TECHNOLOGIES

The technical requirements of communications systems affect the application of cryptographic techniques.

Applying cryptography to communications systems is not always as simple as it may at first appear. Although the basic concepts (see appendix A) still apply as the communications techniques become more involved, the nature of the communications system itself affects its integration with cryptographic techniques. The technical problems can be very complex. A few basic examples will demonstrate these challenges and portray how the technology of the cryptographic systems evolved.

First, consider the simple system shown in the figure at the top of page 72. In this case, the use of the communications path is limited to those parties located at either end. No other parties are involved. Messages sent from node A go only to node B and vice versa. Although the encrypted traffic may pass through other communication nodes, the end-to-end path is dedicated to the primary communicators. Both parties use the same symmetrical, secret-key encryption algorithms. The data are encrypted at node A and decrypted at node B with the same secret key that has been distributed securely prior to the start of the communications process. This is called an end-to-end mode. There are technical problems involved in ensuring that the decryption process uses the key on the ciphertext in exactly the same way (bit-for-bit) that it was used in the encryption process. This is often called crypto synchronization. If the system operates in both directions

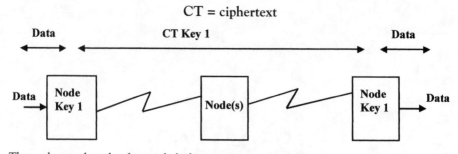

CT = ciphertext

The end-to-end mode of securely linking two communicators

simultaneously, it is called a duplex system, and if it works in only one direction at a time, it is called half-duplex.

In the simplest operational mode, the encrypted messages are sent one at a time, and the link is either not used or operates in an unencrypted mode at other times. While this mode may be satisfactory in many circumstances, it is often desirable to make it difficult for potential eavesdroppers to determine whether a message is being sent. In such cases, random data that cannot be distinguished from real ciphertext are transmitted at all times. This is called traffic-flow security.

While such a system may satisfy security requirements, it may not be an efficient use of the communications path.

A second system type is shown below, still in a much simplified form. In this case, there may be one or more intermediate points in the total communications path, and these points may serve multiple communicators. Suppose a message must be sent from node A to node E via the communications center at node B. The communications system (including the operators) knows where to send the

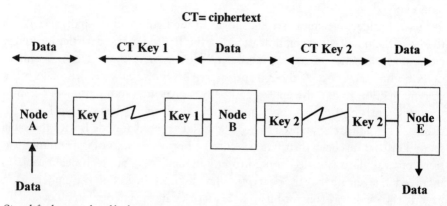

CT= ciphertext

Simplified example of link encryption

message by reading the address if it is unencrypted, but what if the entire message, including the address, is encrypted? One solution is a system that protects the data only between the nodes of the total system; that is, the message and its routing information are decrypted in the relay communications center and retransmitted to the desired recipient. Of course, multiple recipients complicate the situation a bit more. This process of retransmission, or relay, may involve a different cryptographic key than the one used by the original sender. This is called link encryption if the message and routing information is available to people in the relay communications center, and it is called node encryption if the routing activity itself is done in a secure fashion by technical features in the encryption and communications equipment.

In the real world, where mistakes are made and cryptographic keys and other techniques are compromised, the overall security of any such system increases when the cryptographic keys are changed relatively frequently. The definition of "frequently" depends on many factors, including the availability of appropriate technology and the supporting systems surrounding the entire process.

Several major points are worth noting here. First, a communication system with even a modest number of terminals will require a large set of keying material and a methodology for changing the keys throughout the system. Second, some advantage would be gained in incorporating all of the cryptographic functions into a separate subsystem, or box, that could be controlled as sensitive material that is separate from all other parts of the system, particularly if the communications system did not use the same equipment at each node. Third, some coordination between terminals will be required for the system to start up. And fourth, even in the simplest of systems, such as those described here, there is a requirement for some degree of communication between the operators of all parts of the system for maintenance and other operational matters.

Another perhaps less obvious factor is important to the overall security of the system. Certain portions of the total system must be physically protected from the potential eavesdropper. Consider the consequences if an adversary had access to the connections between various parts of the system within the relay communications center. They could conceivably gain access to keying material, or even to the plaintext itself. Consequently, communications centers tend to be some of the best-protected facilities in both military and civilian applications. Without trusted and well-trained employees, no amount of technology will protect the information.

All of these factors, and many others, had an impact of the application of technology to symmetrical, secret-key encryption systems. The government tended to develop the encryption mechanisms—whether based on electromechanical, vacuum-tube, or transistor technology—as separate, physically controlled subsystems that incorporated all aspects of managing the cryptographic functions of the communications system. In military and government systems, the people who operated and maintained the communication systems' cryptographic elements were handpicked and carefully trained; special organizations (i.e., separate from the operating and using elements) also generated and managed the keying of materials. Even during the Civil War, these organizations were not under the control of the users of the communications systems,[1] although the subject was important enough to provoke considerable organizational debate.[2]

Even though cryptography had commercial uses, by the end of World War II, the government held nearly exclusive domain over the bulk of cryptographic equipments. Their application to communication systems could be characterized by the following features:

They were government developed and produced.
They used secret government algorithms.
They were implemented in separate subsystems (i.e., "boxes" with government nomenclatures) and treated as classified material.
They were installed, operated, and controlled by government authorities in designated facilities or as parts of military units.
They required physical contact for keying.

Although a few of these characteristics remain, we shall see the changes wrought by improved technology and the spread of cryptography into many areas of the total marketplace.

Transistors are considered unready for wide-scale use in the period just after World War II.

In the late 1940s, the U.S. government made modernizing and improving its worldwide communications systems a priority. Wartime experience had shown the value of rapid and secure communications, but the equipment was growing old and the wartime networks had not been structured to meet the postwar requirements. A particular need emerged for securely written or "record" communications at many security classification levels. A long-term upgrade of a variety of communications systems was in order. The choices of the technologies to be used in the upgrades presented special problems. A major question was, How soon can the new solid-state technologies be applied?

When engineers defined the postwar government requirements for secure radio-teletype, the most mature electronic technology available to them was the miniature vacuum tube. While tubes had limitations related to their reliability and power consumption, the transistor was judged to be not quite ready for wide-scale use. Yet the need for new equipment could not be delayed. Government engineers sought out leading-edge industrial partners in digital technology to build a new generation of cryptographic equipment.[3]

In cooperation with the Burroughs Corporation, government engineers experimented with multiple winding torroidal magnetic cores known as Bistable Magnetic Elements (BIMAGs). This partnership emerged partly because of Jerry Moskowitz, a young government engineer, who became intrigued with the BIMAGs research of a former college classmate, Lyle Thompson, a Burroughs Corporation Research Center employee. With appropriate interconnections, BIMAGs performed the binary logic and were used to implement shift registers. Funding was provided for further research.

In 1952, the government fabricated an experimental vacuum-tube model, a forerunner of the KW-26, to demonstrate "proof of concept." A common fill device (CFD), used to provide key material for the KW-26, was the first of its kind and represented an important engineering step. The CFD was designed by Charles Napier. It used a key card, an IBM card punched in a RemRand format (45 vice 80 columns, and round rather than rectangular holes). In practice, the operator inserted the daily key card into the CFD and closed the door, securely locking the card in place. For security purposes its physical design limited any given key card to a one-time-only use.

The contract for engineering development models was awarded to the Burroughs Corporation in 1953. The cryptographic logic and the CFD were government furnished. The initial design indicated that BIMAGs were superior to vacuum tubes on reliability and power consumption. Though the KW-26 clock rate was relatively slow, less than 5 khz, the pentode vacuum tubes driving the BIMAG elements were approaching their design limits. A follow-on contract for Final Engineering Development Models was awarded to Burroughs in 1955. Initial deliveries began in 1957 for customer evaluation.

The Burroughs plant in Detroit was awarded the contract for the initial production order in 1958 for about 1,500 units for specific requirements. Orders continued to grow from a variety of service programs, and more than 5,000 were produced. Additional units were purchased by the Defense Communications Agency, the U.S. Department of State, and the Central Intelligence Agency.

A KW-26 system (transmitter or receiver) contained more than eight hundred cores and approximately fifty vacuum-tube driver circuits, occupying slightly more than one-half of a standard relay rack. Most of the space in the rack and most of the 1-kw input power were required for the special-purpose vacuum tube circuits needed to provide compatibility with the multiple input and output circuits.

This milestone cryptographic tool was used for more than twenty years. Using a mix of mature and advanced technologies has an inherent hazard: because some of the latest technologies will be superseded by newer techniques their application

A Navy communications center using the KW-26 System. A communications specialist adjusts one of fourteen KW-26 units in one set of racks in this center. This type of installation was typical for large land-based centers that had good power and air-conditioning equipment. Configurations were many and varied depending on location and circumstances. Reliability was good, although there was a demand for skilled maintenance people. U.S. Navy, courtesy of the Center for Cryptologic History

period will be limited. BIMAGs were in that category. In addition, the miniature vacuum tubes soon became obsolete as the transistor matured. Extraordinary efforts (including special production runs of otherwise obsolete items) were required to support the deployment of the KW-26 over its operational lifetime.

Most conspicuous are the changes in commercial communications brought about by postwar technology. They provided the marketplace for many advanced technologies, and the results became public very quickly.

## August 1951

The first transcontinental telephone call was placed over a microwave relay system (New York to San Francisco).

A multipurpose microwave relay antenna tower. Applications of this radio technique have continued to grow; evidence of this fact exists in all parts of the country. This particular modern installation is typical of many that now support high-capacity telephone and data communications. Note that there are approximately twelve microwave antennas on this tower along with several HF, VHF, and UHF antenna systems.

An ATLAS installation, circa 1954. While this photograph does not show any technical detail of these milestone cryptologic tools, it does serve to illustrate that they were formidable systems. They were not experiments, but were operational systems that were used by both cryptographers and cryptanalysts in their daily work. *Center for Cryptologic History*

## Early 1950s

Major television broadcast standards were adopted in 1952, and public use expanded dramatically worldwide.

Remington Rand, Inc., invested in the design and development activities of Mauchly and Eckert (see chapter 5) and continued to develop what was to become the UNIVAC system. Although the first three systems were sold to the government, including the U.S. Census Bureau, which had been the original sponsor, UNIVAC I became the first commercially marketed computer. It was used, among other things, to support analysis of the 1950 census data and to make early projections on the 1952 presidential election.

Between 1950 and 1954, ERA developed and delivered four advanced computers (two ATLAS Is and two ATLAS IIs) for use by cryptographers. These computers included important innovations such as using magnetic cores for high-speed memory and permitting two-address instructions for the first time.

Remington-Rand eventually bought both EMCC and ERA.

While on duty with the U.S. Navy, Grace Murray Hopper developed the first software compiler, a tool and concept that greatly simplified programming.

Also in this general time period, a team of engineers, including Russell Kirsch at the National Bureau of Standards (NBS), designed and built several large computers using vacuum-tube technology. The first of these was the Standards Electronic Automatic Computer (SEAC). It included a number of innovations including the ability to file share and an early graphical display.

## Mid-1950s

Engineers were encouraged by the success of computer laboratory work at universities, in government, and in industry. This success led to unusual teaming arrangements for the purpose of developing advanced technology equipments for special applications far in advance of their widespread commercial use. The cryptologic community presented challenging requirements and industry responded. This interaction was aided by a healthy exchange of individuals between government and industry. For example, Dr. Howard Engstrom, one of the Navy intelligence specialists who founded ERA, returned to government service in 1956 and

SEAC in operation at the National Bureau of Standards (now the National Institute for Standards and Technology), circa 1955. This advanced capability was made available for a wide variety of research purposes in mathematics, engineering, physics, and chemistry, as well as business and economics. It remained in useful service for thirteen years. *National Institute for Standards and Technology*

was soon appointed as deputy director of the National Security Agency (NSA). In 1958 he returned to work with Remington Rand. Another example is A. B. Clark, who led the development group at BTL that produced SIGSALY. He later led research and development activities of NSA in the mid-1950s.

## 1955

The Sperry Corporation merged with Remington-Rand, forming Sperry-Rand.

## 1956

A number of talented ex-ERA employees left Sperry-Rand and formed the Control Data Corporation (CDC); CDC was formally incorporated in 1957 with William Norris as president. Among the talented staff of ex-ERA employees was the designer Seymour Cray.

The first transatlantic submarine telephone cable (TAT-1) was placed in service in 1956.

Also in this year the Consultative Committee for International Telephone and Telegraph (CCITT) was formed. This committee was intended to serve as a primary technical standards group for international communications activities.

Not surprisingly, the application of solid-state electronics and the revolutionary capabilities of satellite systems continued to accelerate changes in our three fields of interest—communications, computers, and cryptology.

## 1957

The Soviet Union launched Sputnik I, which demonstrated the basic technology of satellite systems.

Also in 1957, but much less conspicuous than the revolutionary achievement of Sputnik I, John Backus and his team at IBM delivered the first Fortran (FORmula TRANslator) compiler. Fortran was the first widely accepted technical programming language.

## 1958

Jack Kilby, an employee of Texas Instruments, filed a patent for what came to be known as the integrated circuit. Similar work by Robert Noyce was in progress at Fairchild Semiconductor. Kilby was awarded the Nobel Prize for his work in 2000.

The first solid-state electronic computer was developed and applied to cryptologic problems.

A good example of industrial teaming on an advanced electronic development program was the 1958 delivery by the Philco Corporation—working with Sperry-

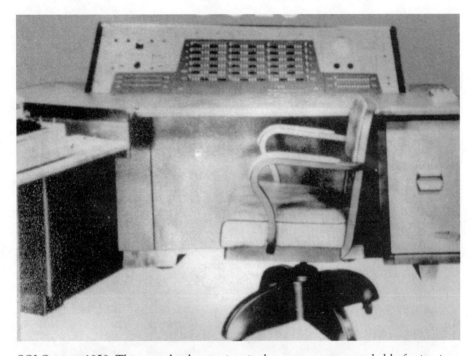

SOLO, circa 1958. This completely transistorized computer was remarkable for its time. Just larger than a normal desk, it was greatly reduced in size and power over comparable hybrid equipment (vacuum tube and transistorized circuits). Although it never went into large production, it was a successful first step in the development of solid-state electronics computers as an aid to cryptologic activities. *Center for Cryptologic History*

Rand, UNIVAC, and Magnetic Controls Corporation—of the desk-sized SOLO, the United States' first completely transistorized computer. It was used at NSA for a variety of purposes.

Dr. Louis W. Tordella became the deputy director of NSA in 1958 and held that position until 1974. Under his guidance and direction, advanced technology products from both the communications and computer industries were rapidly assimilated into all phases of cryptologic activities. In particular, he advocated maintaining close working relationships with most of the emerging computer companies concerning their development of advanced computing capability to ensure that the government cryptologic staff had access to the very best tools available in the world.

The Digital Equipment Corporation (DEC) was founded in 1958, and the computer industry continued to grow.

Dr. Louis Tordella (1911–1996). Soon after obtaining a Ph.D. in mathematics from the University of Illinois, Dr. Tordella became a member of the U.S. Navy's cryptologic unit, OP-20-G, and served in it during World War II. He joined the new Armed Forces Security Agency in 1949. He became NSA's deputy director in 1958 and served in that position until his retirement in 1974. He was a powerful advocate of the use of the most advanced computers in cryptologic work and was responsible for many unique applications. The current NSA supercomputer building is named after Dr. Tordella. *Center for Cryptologic History*

# 1959

A joint defense-industry working group, the Committee on Data System Languages, led by Joe Wegstein of NBS and including Grace Hopper, was formed and created the programming language COBOL (common business-oriented language).

# 1960s

The federal government moved to exploit computers in key areas such as defense, space, and air-traffic control. The U.S. Department of Defense began to develop the World Wide Command and Control System for the control of nuclear weapons in the event of war with the Soviet Union. The National Aeronautics & Space Administration (NASA) acquired special computers to go on board the Apollo spacecraft. The Federal Aviation Administration began to develop an air-traffic control system based on what would become IBM's 360 computer series.

Transistor circuitry also found its way quickly into communications security equipment once reliability data were obtained and good design criteria were established. An example is the KW-7, an all-transistor unit that can be thought of as a replacement for the KW-26. It was deployed initially in the 1960s. The unit was significantly smaller than its predecessors and had much lower power consumption. Workers still inserted keying material into the equipment in much the same way as they did in the KW-26. RCA was a major supplier of the equipment, which was based on NSA-developed and -approved cryptographic algorithms and built to NSA-supplied specifications. Maintaining physical security of keying material remained a major problem in any widely deployed cryptographic equipment.

Transistors were also applied to the problem of voice security. The KY-3 voice encryption system was still too large and power-hungry for graceful tactical field use and was not intended for that purpose, but it did gain acceptance in a wide variety of office-like applications. It was specified in detail by NSA engineers and produced by the Bendix Corporation. The KY-3 used an encoding process known as Pulse Code Modulation (PCM), which permitted high-quality speech reproduction but required transmission of a 50,000 bit per second (50 kb) signal. The standard telephone circuits of that time could not handle signals with such large bandwidth. Consequently, special (and expensive) systems were necessary for point-to-point transmission of the signal. This transmission capacity limitation relegated the KY-3 to a restricted set of users. However, it was capable of full-duplex operation and could produce good-quality voice. In the proper environment, the handset could be separated from the base unit (which weighed approximately three hundred pounds), but the entire system was protected as classified information. Although it was not easy to maintain, in some locations the system remained in use until the late 1980s.

## 1960

Digital Equipment Corporation (DEC) introduced the PDP-1, which included a large cathode ray tube for graphics display purposes.

The first laser was demonstrated. Based on a 1958 paper, *Infrared and Optical Lasers* by Arthur Schawlow of BTL and Charles Townes of Columbia University, this multipurpose invention offered many new opportunities in communications and other fields.[4] Both inventors remained active in physics and each would win (along with others) a Nobel Prize for this and related work (Townes in 1964 and Schawlow in 1981).

## 1961

IBM delivered the first STRETCH computer to Los Alamos, New Mexico. The development contract had been awarded in 1956. For at least three years, STRETCH was the world's fastest computer.

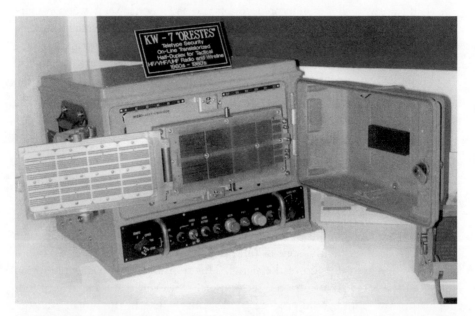

The KW-7 data encryption system. This transistorized unit was about one foot wide. The general construction of the CFD is shown here. Key cards were inserted between the contact plates. Once inserted they could not be reused. This type of unit was used in a wide variety of applications. *J. V. Boone in the National Cryptologic Museum*

The KY-3 voice ciphony system. This transistorized unit looked much like a safe. Although it was hardly portable and required costly communications connections, it was widely deployed and served its primary purpose for many years. *Center for Cryptologic History*

Also this year, the IBM 1301 Disk Storage unit was introduced. This technology had been introduced in 1954 by J. J. Hagopian and was the first high-speed random access disk file.

Leonard Kleinrock of MIT produced the first detailed paper on packet-switching theory. This accomplishment was an important stepping-stone toward the development of the modern Internet.

## 1962

Several groups demonstrated the first semiconductor laser diodes. These devices would soon be applied in a wide variety of system applications.

As an example of large-scale computer engineering, in fewer than four years of development time, IBM delivered HARVEST to cryptologists in 1962. HAR-

A view of the HARVEST operating area, February 1962. Although this staged photograph shows a rather sterile scene, in actual operation the HARVEST system was at the center of a very busy operations area. The mechanical actions of the unique magnetic tape drives, the operations of the large printers, and the general activities of the operating personnel gave the area its own dynamic personality. *Center for Cryptologic History*

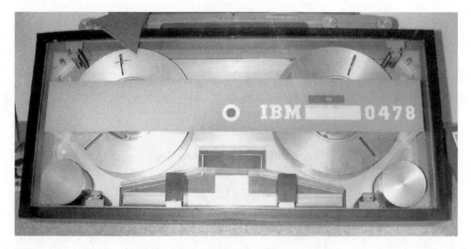

Magnetic tape cartridge from HARVEST. This large magnetic tape cartridge, which many believe to be the forerunner of modern tape transports, was incorporated into a sub-system of HARVEST called TRACTOR. A single cartridge was about two feet long and weighed several pounds. The magnetic tape was about two inches wide. The TRACTOR system was a mechanical marvel that automatically loaded and unloaded tape cartridges from the tape readers. This was the latest technique for rapid access to large volumes of stored data.

VEST was a system based on the IBM STRETCH computer. STRETCH was the world's fastest computer and had first been delivered to Los Alamos in the previous year for research on atomic energy problems. The HARVEST system used automated, high-capacity, high-speed, magnetic tape external storage units for the first time on a large scale. The system used about 160 tape cartridges with a capability to store about 88 billion characters. The transfer rate was more than one million characters per second. This complex system was operational for many years at NSA and heavily influenced the design of the subsequent IBM System 360.

## 1963

The Semi-Automatic Ground Environment (SAGE) air defense system became fully operational and was the first large-scale computer/communications network. It used the AN/FSQ-7 computer, which had been developed at MIT as the fundamental computing element. It was deployed at more than 100 interconnected sites and accepted commands by the operators interacting directly with the cathode ray tube (CRT) displays.

Advances in satellite relay and cable technology provided entirely new capabilities to communicate. When combined with continuing improvements in other areas and advances in basic electronics, these advances meant that additional means of long-distance transmission of voice, data, and images were introduced at a rapid pace.

## May 1963

Telstar I, developed by BTL, became the first active-relay communications satellite.

## July 1963

Syncom 2 was the first geosynchronous satellite demonstration. This step opened up the potential for high-capacity radio-frequency information transmission on a truly worldwide basis.

## 1964

Transpacific cable telephone service began. The Communications Satellite (COMSAT) Corporation, authorized by Congress in 1962, was formally incorporated for the purpose of developing public satellite communications systems. In 1964, an additional seventeen countries joined COMSAT in forming the International Telecommunications Satellite Consortium (Intelsat). This was an important step in creating a global communications satellite system.

IBM announced the System/360 family of computers. The System/360 family ranged from small, relatively cheap computers to large and expensive systems all of which used the same basic software and were compatible with each other. Among other things, this step enabled many peripheral devices to be shared among multiple computers. The huge demand for this system made IBM the leader in the electronic computer market.

Also in 1964, CDC introduced the 6600 Supercomputer. This system, designed by Seymour Cray, could execute three million instructions per second, which was at least three times faster than any other computer at that time. It incorporated the ability to use peripheral processors, which managed the data transfer to a central processing system.

## 1965

DEC introduced their PDP-8, the first commercially successful minicomputer—an important step in moving computing capability into manufacturing and scientific laboratories without large capital investments.

John Kenny and Tom Kurtz of Dartmouth developed BASIC, a programming language intended primarily for students.

## Mid-1960s

In both government and industry laboratories, efforts continued in the development of equipment that could solve the speech-quality versus available-bandwidth problem represented by the KY-3. Some of the efforts focused on trying low-rate digital encoding of the voice signal prior to encryption. Engineers developed and deployed some equipment that met the bandwidth requirements, but none were completely successful. Only the most determined of communicators would use the systems regularly.

Other attempts to solve the problem involved complex scrambling techniques of the analog voice signal rather than digitizing and then digitally encrypting. Concerns emerged that these analog-scrambling techniques would not present a sufficient challenge to an adversary's cryptanalytic capability, but in the end the complex scrambling techniques caused degradation in the original signal with a resulting loss of speech quality at the receiving terminal. Some systems were built and deployed in both surface and airborne versions, but they were not accepted into wide use. The technology challenges remained.

NSA engineers worked with their industry counterparts to develop a family of components that could address the voice-encryption problem by using an early version of integrated circuits. While these building block components incorporated only fifteen to twenty transistors on a chip, they were the forerunners of greater things to come. They were used in a family of tactical radio encryptors called NESTOR.

NESTOR included a "manpackable" equipment called the KY-38 and a compatible airborne version called the KY-28. They used a PCM voice encoding technique that operated at about 19 kb and could be used with existing VHF and UHF tactical radios. Although problems with voice quality persisted, this equipment did represent a significant improvement in size, weight, and power consumption.

Because the KY-38 was still too heavy for one soldier to carry along with the radio and the associated battery packs, two-person teams were required for communications purposes. The KY-38 was a significant advancement, but the weight factor along with the low quality of the voice made it clear that further improvements were needed. The improvements would depend on the application of more advanced Large Scale Integration (LSI) to the electronics subassemblies.

This time period also made clear the need for the ability to encrypt television signals. The analog television signal of the time had to be converted into a digital format to be suitable for high-grade encryption. As in the case of the voice signal, the digitization process increased the bandwidth required for transmission of the enciphered signal. In response to this challenge, the Philco Corporation, in conjunction with the Ball Brothers Corporation, developed television signal encoding equipment that used a special encoding algorithm that provided a 40 mb representation of the analog television signal. This equipment maintained the potential for high-quality video even after transmission and the encryption/decryption process. Now the problem was that there was no routine way to perform the encryption and decryption at the required rates.

NSA awarded a development contract to RCA to address this issue. A primary problem was that most of the transistors of the day did not operate at the required speed, and those that did were very expensive. The speed problem was solved by development of a technique that would today be called parallel processing. The input 40 mb signal was separated into two parallel 20 mb streams. These streams were separately encrypted and then recombined into a 40 mb serial stream for transmission. This technique allowed the use of the slower, less expensive transistors for the majority of the equipment; the high-speed devices were required only for the input and output circuits. The equipment was given the nomenclature of the KG-24.

The KG-24 worked and was deployed. However, it was still large (occupying a five-foot-high cabinet) and it was still expensive. As a result, the systems that were fielded were placed only in limited operation in the White House, the Pentagon, and similar high-level locations.

## 1967

Fairchild Camera and Instrument Company built the first standard microelectronics chip intended for data processing. It contained an 8-bit arithmetic unit and an accumulator.

The Simula 67 programming language, invented by Ole-Johan Dahl and Kirsten Nygaard of the Norwegian Computing Center in Oslo, Norway, was the first object-oriented programming language.

In the realm of communications systems, 1997 saw the initial Defense Satellite Communications System (DSCS), consisting of twenty-six satellites in low earth orbit, placed into operation as a research and development program. This constellation was replaced with the DSCS II series of synchronous systems starting in 1974.

## 1968

AT&T proposed the concept of cellular mobile communications systems to the FCC. This proposal would have a significant impact on communications once cellular technology became available.

The science fiction writer Arthur C. Clarke and film director Stanley Kubrick partnered to produce the futuristic motion picture *2001: A Space Odyssey*. A main character on board was a supercomputer in charge of a spacecraft mission to the planet Jupiter. The computer was a projection of advanced artificial intelligence capability and was called HAL. HAL is perhaps a substitution cipher of IBM, but its name was reputed to be based on "heuristic" and "algorithmic" methods of learning. The conflicts between the humans and the computer in the conduct of the mission probably stimulated the imaginations of many students. As a somewhat curious testimony to the wide impact of this movie, in 2003 HAL was selected by the American Film Institute to be thirteenth among the fifty most famous villains in American movie history.

Most of the technological, industrial, and regulatory tools were now in place to permit continued expansion of communications and computational capabilities. Only one area was retarding this advancement—cryptologic key management.

# 7

# 1970–2003:
# EXTENDED NETWORKING
# CONCEPTS BRING CLOSER
# INTEGRATION TO ALL
# THREE TECHNOLOGIES

Until the late 1960s, the primary operational weak link in any cryptographic system was the difficulty of maintaining the integrity of the keying material. This weakness limited cryptography applications in large networks.

Despite elaborate security precautions, training, and inspections and audits, the secrecy of keying material has sometimes been compromised. A well-known example is the infamous Walker spy ring of the cold war era that delivered keying material to the Soviets, which put many U.S. Navy operations at risk.[1] Beyond security concerns was the high cost of maintaining a complex transportation system for distributing keying material to systems deployed all over the world. Many engineers took on the challenge of finding a way to solve these serious problems. One who succeeded was Howard E. Rosenblum of NSA.

In early 1969, Rosenblum was awarded a secret patent (declassified in the early 1980s) that described the concept for what came to be called electronic key distribution. It was designed to work within what were termed symmetrical, secret-key cryptographic systems. This concept incorporated secure communications into the very center of the process of securing the communications on a larger scale. Much as the telegraph and Morse code had separated communications from transportation in the mid-1800s, the electronic distribution of cryptographic keys via key distribution centers (KDC) separated cryptographic keys from transportation systems. It was a major breakthrough. The basic principles are still in use today.

In the same general timeframe, James Ellis, a mathematician at the British Government Communications Headquarters (GCHQ), examined the key management system in a different way. He entertained the theoretical possibility that a system of encryption might be devised that did not require the communicating parties to exchange secret keys in advance of establishing secure communications. He called it "non-secret encryption." An essential part of his idea depended on the existence of nonreversible mathematical functions.[2] If the proper functions could be found, then an entirely new scheme of cryptography would exist. Further work at GCHQ by Clifford Cox and Malcolm Williamson produced the theory for a practical system in 1973. The ideas remained classified and were not implemented. However, what is now known as public-key cryptography had been invented, even if only a few people, all dedicated to secrecy, knew about it. It would soon appear in the public domain in the United States.

The advent of satellite systems in the late 1960s also presented new challenges. Securing the command-and-control functions of a satellite system is no easy matter. Their very nature makes them visible to anyone who is properly equipped. In addition, the systems are expensive, have long lifetimes (hopefully), are not usually subject to repair or replacement, and are subjected to the harsh radiation environment of space, as well as a challenging launch environment. Cryptographic techniques offer solutions to many of the problems inherent in the command and control of satellites. In particular, they offer means to authenticate commands and, as an added advantage, they can be used to protect the distribution of the data collected by the satellite system either from its sensors or from its internal instrumentation (telemetry).

Long-term programs were established to develop radiation-hardened electronics for spacecraft applications and to apply them quickly to command and control systems through dedicated encryption subsystems that could be used on a variety of applications. In this case, a special type of keying system was developed that had the useful characteristic of limiting the propagation of errors in the communications systems on occasions where, for one reason or another, it might lose synchronization. It was called Cypher Text Auto Key (CTAK).[3] The KG-28 (see photo on page 94) was the first space-qualified system to use this technique. It was introduced in the late 1960s and produced by Motorola.

# 1970

The first publication of the Host-Host protocol for ARPANET, the Defense Department's Advanced Research Project Agency's (ARPA) research program on internetworking, appeared, and the first cross-country link was installed using the protocol.

Intel Corporation produced the first general-purpose microprocessor and named it the 4004. The 4004 was a 4-bit central processor that was used as part of a four-chip set and used 2,300 transistors. The microprocessor was a milestone event in computer systems because it enabled designers to rely on existing integrated circuits to perform the basic functions of the actual processing and computing. These integrated circuits contained the entire central processing capability of the design in an economical unit, leaving the data storage, display, timing, and other functions to be added as requirements demanded. All manner of innovative applications followed.

Also in this year, Dennis Ritchie and Kenneth Thomson led the development effort at BTL of the UNIX operating system. This system found wide application and was the standard for many years.

The programming language "C" was developed to work with UNIX.

About this time practical optical fibers were developed after years of experimental and developmental work in the United States, England, and Japan. In the United States, BTL and Corning were heavily involved. This development, coupled with advancements in laser diodes (see 1972 on page 95), promised the potential for

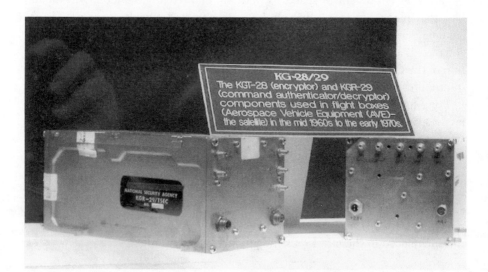

The KGT-28 (or simply KG-28) and the KGA-29 were two of the first space-qualified encryption equipments. The latter was used as a command authenticator/decryptor for space missions, and the former was used for the encryption of mission data and telemetry. Both of these units proved to be highly reliable as a result of their unique designs, extensive testing, and the use of radiation-hardened electronics. They were remarkably small and lightweight and used little power, all of which made them suitable for satellite use.

high-capacity data transmission over long distances and would eventually offer a competitive option to radio-frequency carrier systems in some applications.

## January 1971

Intelsat 4 (flights F2 and F3) began the first regular commercial phone and television relay service via satellite from positions over the Atlantic Ocean. These two were joined in 1972 by F4 over the Pacific and F5 over the Indian Ocean. Together they could provide a maximum of nine thousand channels of voice telephony or twelve channels of color television. Hughes Aircraft Company was the spacecraft prime contractor in a team that was made up of twelve major suppliers from ten countries.

## November 1971

Intel released the first microprocessor for general commercial sales.

Continued improvements in LSI circuit technology and in voice encoding techniques led to the development of another family of tactical voice security equipment. This generation was called VINSON. The ground and airborne versions employed a new voice encoding technique called Continuous Variable Slope Delta (CVSD) modulation that operated at 16 Kbits and provided much improved voice quality over the PCM system that was used in NESTOR. The resulting systems, called the KY-57 and -58, also incorporated an electronic rekeying system. The combined three new stages of technological developments resulted in a much wider acceptance of the units in the field. Many thousands of units of this equipment were deployed in the 1970s and 1980s. It had taken time and sustained efforts in both government and industry, but technology had met at least the basic requirements of this cryptologic marketplace.

## 1972

The first demonstration of high-speed (1 Gigabit/sec) modulation of a laser diode took place at Standard Telecommunication Laboratories in England. This was followed by advancements in device lifetimes and, coupled with development of fiber-optic cables, opened up the commercial use of this transmission medium.

Hewlett-Packard introduced the HP-35 Pocket Calculator in 1972. The first to perform a variety of mathematical functions and to store the solutions for further use, the HP-35 found wide application in a growing marketplace. Also in this year the Palo Alto Research Center (PARC) of Xerox demonstrated ALTO, a computer that first used the mouse and an on-screen graphical interface.

Nolan Bushnell introduced PONG, the first computer game.

Intelsat 4 under test, circa 1970. This spin-stabilized geosynchronous satellite carried the communications subsystem on a mechanically despun platform supporting two 50-inch-diameter dishes and a cluster of other antennae. The cylinder spun at approximately sixty revolutions per minute, was 111 inches tall, and was covered with solar cells that produced more than 500 watts of power. The spacecraft weighed more than 1,500 pounds in the on-orbit configuration. The satellite is shown here being readied for test in an anechoic chamber. *Northrop-Grumman Space Technology*

The personal computer would not be introduced until much later in the decade, but microprocessors and the potential for relatively small computers were making clear the need for a standard method of encryption to support emerging data processing structures in banking and other commercial applications. By 1973 the National Bureau of Standards (NBS) publicly solicited proposals for such a standard.

IBM researchers were already at work on developing a versatile cryptrographic product, intending to sell it as a proprietary item. Many people were associated with this development with Horst Feistel, Alan Kronheim, Walter Tuchman, and Carl Meyer having key roles. The product would be for symmetrical, secret-key systems, and since public use was the goal, the entire security of the system depended on maintaining the secrecy of the key.

IBM officials decided to offer their work to NBS. There was considerable activity and discussion among all the parties concerning factors such as government certification and export controls, but in 1975 NBS selected the IBM design as the Data Encryption Standard (DES). For the first time, the U.S. government had first solicited, then endorsed and promulgated a technical standard for secure public cryptographic uses.

## 1973

The specific Internet problem was addressed by Robert Kahn of ARPA and Vinton Cerf of Stanford University. This work and the resulting protocol named TCP/IP permitted various kinds of packet-switched networks to interact and was a key part of the ARPANET. President Clinton presented these Internet pioneers with the National Medal of Technology in December 1997.

## 1974

Not all of the government's work in this time period focused directly on the basic technology fields. In 1974, recognizing pervasive information collection and processing by both government and industry and provoked in part by the Watergate scandals, Congress passed Public Law 98-579, known as the Privacy Act of 1974. This law took effect in late 1975 and was characterized by the U.S. Department of Justice in 2002 as "an omnibus code of fair information practices that attempts to regulate the collection, maintenance, use and dissemination of personal information by federal executive branch agencies. However, the Act's imprecise language, limited legislative history and somewhat outdated regulatory guidelines have rendered it a difficult statute to decipher and apply."[4]

Those who have tried to implement the act probably agree that this is an unusual, but appropriate, use of the word "decipher." However, this law did provoke serious responses, among them the publication by the U.S. Department of Commerce of Federal Information Processing Standards' Publication 41 in May 1975. It is entitled *Computer Security Guidelines for Implementing the Privacy Act of 1974.* Among many other things this publication presents the DES as "background information for the planners of future networks." It has become much more than that.

IBM, NBS, several review groups, and NSA had cooperated in the selection and analysis process. Many individuals believed that the DES had built-in flaws (or "backdoors") that would allow easy decryption by knowledgeable government cryptanalysts. Much acrimonious debate ensued. However, DES (in several versions) went almost immediately into wide use and has remained useful for decades.[5]

The introduction of expanded networking considerations promoted many additional applications. Once telecommunications were no longer experimental, it became clear that dedicating communications paths to more than a few potential communicators was not possible. We have all seen pictures of the old telephone-switching centers where operators took verbal requests from customers and manually plugged the connections into place. Progress has been rapid. Some of us have actually seen those centers. Others remember the party lines of the 1940s where neighbors essentially shared phone lines and depended on the particular ring of the operator to identify which party was being called. The demand for connectivity has always been high. The ability of technology and system designers to deliver that connectivity began to match the demand in the 1960s and 1970s. The term "network" came into wide use in this general period.

What is a "network"? One good basic definition is "a network consists essentially of network switches, or nodes, interconnected by transmission links. These links can be wire, cable, radio, satellite, or fiber-optics facilities."[6]

Network designers must consider all of the issues in providing the desired connections that are timely, reliable, and technically compatible. They must also provide the mechanisms to ensure accurate and recognizable transmitted information at the receiving end of the communications path. Perhaps if all of the communications paths of the world had come into being at one time this process would be simpler, but in fact the total communications capability of nations (whether military or commercial) is a constantly evolving collection of individual parts. (See chapter 4 for a brief discussion of the challenges of securing networks.)

With the obvious advantages of communicating from system to system, nation to nation, business to business, network to network, and, yes, military service to service, governments have established sets of protocols (or rules) to guide system designers and operators. An elaborate set of international organizations manages this process. Their success depends on many factors; technology is only one them. Nevertheless, technology is a key factor in the development of networks, and the spread of networking has again led to new applications that, in turn, further expand the number of communications services.

## 1974

Intel introduced the 8080 microprocessor, which was an 8-bit processor with five thousand transistors and ran about twenty times faster than the four-year-old 4004. It was probably the first microprocessor to find wide use in a variety of applications.

The U.S. Department of Justice filed antitrust actions against the Bell System. This move started protracted legal actions led by William F. Baxter and carried out under the supervision of U.S. District Judge Harold H. Greene. In many ways this action had as much effect on the communications industry as did many important technology innovations.

## Mid-1970s

As the marketplace for advanced computing capability expanded, industrial competition became the driving force for high-speed computing. The government technical community began to concentrate on integrating the most advanced commercial systems into government systems. There were also important activities in the public sector on the cryptographic side of the communications security issues as well. An important and challenging problem like that of key distribution and management attracts technical talent. In 1975 a young researcher at Stanford University, Whitfield Diffie, completely unaware of the British work and driven by strong beliefs regarding the public's right to privacy, invented his own version of a public-key system. He shared his ideas with Martin Hellman and together they developed the technical basis of public-key cryptography and submitted their ideas for publication by the Institute of Electrical and Electronic Engineers (IEEE) under the title of "New Dimensions in Cryptography" in 1976.

Public-key cryptography was now truly public although this new technology would have a long and often highly adversarial path to the marketplace as government, industry, and university authorities often had strong, opposing views about the general public's use of cryptographic techniques.[7] However, a practical implementation of the nonreversible (or one-way) mathematical function was still missing.

Three innovative researchers at the MIT Laboratory of Computer Science soon created a practical implementation of the public-key system. It was published in an internal technical memo in April 1977. The authors were Ronald Rivest, Adi Shamir, and Leonard Adleman; their contribution came to be known as the RSA algorithm. This algorithm is based on the fact that it is extremely difficult (an understatement) to factor large numbers.[8] They created their large number by multiplying large prime numbers and, for practical purposes, a nonreversible mathematical function had now been found. Further, their system could be implemented in the semiconductor technology of the time. Now, not only was public-key cryptography public, it was practical.

Despite continued arguments about export controls and other concerns, communication and computer design teams could now consider approaches that did not require correspondents to exchange secret data prior to engaging in secure message exchanges. This advance did not exempt communicators from meeting technical and procedural requirements, but the existence of these design options made a great impact in both industries. The marketplace was still limited, and arguments between industry and government continued. However, when networked communications began to expand and the capability of personal computers increased, the Internet expanded and the public market for cryptography emerged. Public cryptography of several types became an unavoidable fact by the mid-1990s. That is a good example of a nonreversible economic function.

The early GCHQ work was declassified in 1997. By that time commercial public-key systems of various types were widespread, forming an essential part of the foundation for secure electronic data exchange over the Internet.

The mid-1970s also saw work continue on more satisfactory ways to provide secure voice communications. The human voice creates a very complex signal processing problem for engineers. If transmission bandwidth was always unlimited, perhaps the advent of high-speed very large scale integration (VLSI) analog-to-digital converters would have made it practical to digitize the voice waveform, use some exotic encryption algorithm, and eventually reconstruct the sound of the human voice on the receiving end. However, restricted bandwidth remained a practical problem in many applications for both technical and economic reasons. Work on improved voice encoding continued, and many groups made important contributions.

A research group at NSA that included Joseph Campbell Jr., Thomas Tremain, Mary Kohler, and Richard Dean was particularly focused on the array of problems associated with providing secure voice capability to a wide variety of users. In cooperation with researchers at BTL, they eventually began to focus on adapting a technique called linear predictive coding (LPC) for the next generation of voice coders. Real-time computer simulations were developed, and specialized microelectronic signal processors were soon available for this purpose.

Work continued and an improvement called Code Excited Linear Prediction (CELP) was producing excellent results at a 4.8 kbs output rate. This eventually resulted in the establishment of Federal Standard 1016 for voice processing in the early 1990s.[9] This technique uses an 8 kHz sampling rate and performs a variety of functions that are intended to ensure that the peculiar qualities of human speech are identified and properly coded prior to any other operation (such as encryption) being performed on the data. The technique also enables accurate reproduction of the speech. It is one of several milestones in the ongoing research into speech coding, but it played a particularly important role in enabling the newest generation of voice security systems. In the civil world, a modified CELP coder is used as the basis of the speech processing algorithms in the digital cellular telephone systems now used all across North America.

## 1975

Altair marketed a computer kit for electronic hobbyists. It used the Intel 8080 as the processor and was largely responsible for coining the term "personal com-

The first "personal computer." The manufacturing company MITS produced this kit, which met unexpected success. The basic kit sold for about $300 and came with a 256-bit memory. It received wide publicity from a cover article in *Popular Electronics* magazine. The original owners sold out, and the kits were produced for about three years by Pertec. *Computer History Museum*

puter." Bill Gates and Paul Allen licensed BASIC as the software. The demand exceeded all expectations.

## 1976

Seymour Cray had left CDC and formed his own company. It produced the CRAY-1 supercomputer, which set new standards for speed and capacity. The design was based on vector processing which was an important advancement in computer design. The machine was capable of 100 million floating point operations per second (MFLOPS) and operated on 64-bit words. The initial customers were the Atomic Energy Commission and NSA.

The CRAY-1 family of supercomputers were quickly assimilated into a number of cryptologic systems (and other computer-intensive government programs as well).

## 1977

Steve Wozniak and Steve Jobs were responsible for the design of the widely successful Apple II personal computer. Associated with easy-to-use software and color graphics, it also opened a wide business market. Bill Gates and Paul Allen started their new company, Microsoft.

In an important milestone in communications technology, fiber-optic cables were first used in commercial telephone service by the Bell System in Chicago, Illinois.

## 1978

DEC introduced the VAX 11/780, which was constructed to allow the use of very large (up to 4.3 gigabites) virtual memory. This feature exceeded the capacity of most minicomputers by hundreds of times.

The first Fleet Satellite Communications (FLTSATCOM) satellite was launched into synchronous orbit in 1978 and was followed by other launches in 1979, 1980, and 1981. This system provided near-global continuous UHF and SHF communications for high-priority military units as well as service for the presidential communications network. TRW Inc. was the spacecraft prime contractor, and system program management was provided by the Naval Electronics System Command and the U.S. Air Force Space Division.

## Late 1970s

Secure voice communications continued to be a high priority for the nation's civilian and military leaders. There was a new emphasis on good voice quality, reliability, lower unit cost, and ease of installation and use. In addition to the discovery of

Seymour Cray (1925–1996). A World War II soldier who was a 1950 graduate of the University of Minnesota in electrical engineering, where he also earned a master's degree in applied mathematics, Cray worked at ERA on its advanced computer projects, was one of the founders of CDC, and was the founder of Cray Research. Although he was also a corporate manager, his continuing personal design contributions made a significant difference in the development of advanced computers. He led pioneering work in vector processing designs, specialized mechanisms for cooling and packaging, and the use of reduced instruction set computer chips. *Computer History Museum*

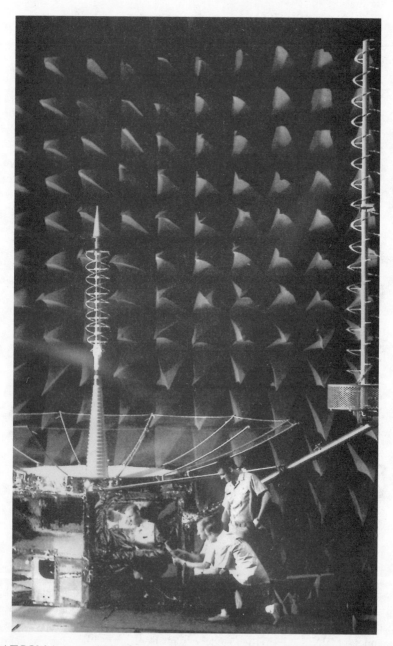

FLTSATCOM 1, circa 1977. The first of the FLTSATCOM series of geostationary communications satellites undergoes tests in an anechoic chamber. The satellite weighed about 2,200 pounds on orbit and the solar arrays, which supplied a minimum of 1.2 kilowatts of power, measured more than 43 feet tip-to-tip. *Northrop-Grumman Space Technology*

the mathematical basis for public-key cryptography (mentioned earlier), advances in semiconductor processing capabilities continued to improve, and it became possible to place thousands, then tens of thousands, of transistors and other elements on a single semiconductor chip. This became commonly known as VLSI. VLSI technology made it possible to perform the extensive calculations required by such systems in an economical manner and the advances in voice coding techniques were also maturing. The combination of these technological developments made it possible to take the next step in secure voice; it was called the STU-III.

Although there had been improvements in voice security systems since the KY-3, the combined set of new requirements were clearly demanding a new generation of equipment. The STU-III was the answer. It would incorporate the progress made in voice encoding, key distribution, and VLSI technology. The goal was to have a cost-effective desk unit (unclassified) that could be used as a normal telephone until there was a need to "go secure." At that time a unique physical key would be inserted into the unit and an electronic system of cryptographic key generation and exchange would be established between the communicating instruments. Relatively large demand for the units was anticipated, and wide use of commercial technology and production techniques was determined appropriate. It was a challenge, but three companies, Motorola, AT&T, and GE/RCA, received production contracts.

The advent of public-key cryptography did not curtail the government's use of the more traditional special-purpose cryptographic equipment. Evolving communication capability did however require that many of the cryptographic systems in current use be replaced. A series of upgrade activities was undertaken also using VLSI technology. The KG-84 family of equipment was typical of this effort. The goals included improved reliability, much-improved system flexibility, and the ability to accommodate new keying techniques. Again, the development was initiated and managed by NSA engineers. Production of the units took place at TRW Inc., Honeywell, and RCA. Deployment started in the early 1980s, and production ended about a decade later.

For example, it could operate on teletypewriter-like information at rates between 50 and 9,600 bits per second in non-synchronous modes and up to 64 Kb in some synchronized modes. It was designed to interface with a variety of communication systems, using their varying transmission rules (or protocols), in both encryption and decryption modes. Another important feature was that the unit itself could be treated as unclassified (yet still controlled by special inventory techniques) when it was not "keyed." Once keyed, it took on the classification of the key being used. This family of equipment was a big step forward; it met its major objectives.

The multipurpose KG-84. This compact unit was the first to take advantage of major applications of VLSI electronics. As a result, it found use in a wide variety of applications. It also proved to be reliable and easy to use and maintain.

## 1979

WordStar, the first word processor, was released.

## 1980

The rate of progress in semiconductor processing made it clear that the next decade would see millions of transistors on a single chip. Therefore, system designers moved beyond the boundaries of constructing microprocessors and started to place more total system functionality on a chip. New design techniques and tools were required. Carver Mead and Lynn Conway put it this way in their 1980 book, *Introduction to VLSI Systems:* "VLSI electronics presents a challenge, not only to those involved in the development of fabrication technology, but also to computer scientists and computer architects. The ways in which digital systems are structured, the procedures used to design them, the trade-offs between hardware and software, and the design of computational algorithms will all be greatly affected by the coming changes in integrated electronics. We believe this will be a major area of activity in computer science on through the 1980s."[10]

They were absolutely right, and the impact was not limited to computer science. As new computer aided design tools began to evolve and new semiconductor materials were introduced, all manner of electronic functions became imbedded in the design of single chips. These functions were eventually not limited to digital signal processing but also included radio-frequency amplification and switching functions.

Communications technologies and computer technologies were drawn even closer together. Signaling System Seven was adopted by the CCITT and began to be deployed. This international standard separates the system management information from the communications channel and promotes the use of new network strategies. This step was made practical by the advances in VLSI technologies.

Alan Shugart founded Shugart Associates and introduced the first hard drive for personal computers.

## 1981

IBM entered the personal computer market with its PC (personal computer). Created by Don Estridge, David Bradley, and others, it used the new Intel 8088 microprocessor and provided 16-bit capability at nearly a 5-Mhz clock rate. Microsoft provided the operating system.

## 1982

As a result of more than six years of legal action, AT&T agreed early this year to divest itself of approximately three-quarters of its assets and restructure the public telephone business into seven regional companies. This action was to have a huge effect on the future of telecommunications in the United States.

The CRAY XMP was introduced and ran at more than 400 MFLOPS. Because of the parallel nature of the processing system, the defense and scientific community developed the capability to use several of these machines simultaneously on the same problem.

As the cryptographic techniques of the world became more complex, cryptanalysts continued to employ the most powerful computational tools that could be made available. The CRAY XMP was the world's most powerful computer in this time period, and it was put on display in the National Cryptologic Museum when

CRAY XMP on display at the National Cryptologic Museum. This central processor unit illustrates the unique mechanical design of this series of CRAY computers. The cylindrical design permitted close control over the electrical connections within the processing unit and also supported an efficient cooling technique. The bench-like lower level is a part of the cooling system. Computers of this type are not stand-alone units; a large amount of support area is required for input and output devices as well as cooling and electrical power conditioning. *Center for Cryptologic History*

the museum opened in the mid-1990s—a great example of the steady march of technology. From "most powerful in the world" to "museum artifact" in less than a decade! Undoubtedly there were also other state-of-the art computers produced by CDC, DEC, IBM, and others in use as well.

Also late in 1982 Compaq introduced the first IBM-compatible portable PC, thereby expanding the marketplace and prompting many new applications.

# 1983

The Defense Communications Agency and the ARPA chose TCP/IP as their standard transmission protocol, specifically dealing with networking of packet networks, for ARPANET, which was now a high-speed network connecting a wide variety of computing and communication centers across the United States. The prototype of the modern Internet was now in place.

The FCC allocated spectrum occupancy for the U.S. Advanced Mobile Phone System (AMPS). Deployment of this cellular system followed quickly with the first U.S. service, which was installed in Chicago.

# 1984

The restructuring of AT&T was officially completed at the start of this year.

The number of Internet hosts exceeded one thousand, and the number of cellular telephone users was estimated to be about twenty-five thousand in the United States.

# 1985

David Deutsch of Oxford published *Quantum Theory, the Church-Turing Principle, and the Universal Quantum Computer*, which opened up an entirely new theoretical approach to performing fast computations involving large numbers. By the year 2000, this field, dubbed "quantum computing," received wide attention. Much progress had been made; however, it was not yet clear where the research would lead or when any usable technology would be assembled into an advanced computing capability. What was clear: if computing devices using this approach became practical, the entire field of advanced computing would be revolutionized.[11] The topic attracted the attention of many researchers.

A group of teenagers in Milwaukee, Wisconsin, electronically broke into a computer at Los Alamos National Laboratory and the resulting publicity produced anxiety among Internet users about hackers.

# Mid-1980s

STU-IIIs began to be deployed in significant numbers. A number of creative organizations had been involved in the development including the Navy and the Treasury Departments. They were informed and ready for the new capability. Between 1987 and 1994 more than three hundred thousand units were produced and deployed. The public-key cryptography infrastructure developed by NSA and its industry partners to support the worldwide deployment of STU-III units was, at one time, the largest in the world.

A production unit of the STU-III secure office telephone. This desk telephone is all that the user of the system ever sees. In addition to providing secure communications capability that includes notifying the users of the highest classification that can be used over the link, the equipment can also be used as a regular telephone over the standard public telephone system. The unit itself, while valuable, can be treated as unclassified equipment when it is "unkeyed." The physical key that is used to initiate a secure connection is visible on the right of the unit. Once communications have been established by using the telephone unit in a conventional manner, the users may "go secure" by inserting their unique keys into their terminals and turning them much as they would do to engage a physical lock. The keys have internal electronic programmable read-only memories that contain a variety of information that enables the network to identify the users and initiate the security features of the telephone. These keys must be physically protected although the exact level of protection is determined by the level of classification that is to be associated with the terminal and its authorized users.

## Mid- to Late 1980s

The Thinking Machine Corporation deployed the massively parallel Connection Machine, which used sixteen thousand individual processors, each with a small memory and linked together in a way that permitted extremely fast computations on many classes of problems. Another world-class machine of a different design

The MISTE II Integrated Satellite Communications Terminal. This type of secure communications equipment was available for military use during Operation Desert Storm and Desert Shield in the early 1990s. Even more advanced versions are available today and support a variety of data types.

than the CRAY series of computers, it was quickly employed at NSA. An example of this computer was removed from service and displayed in the National Cryptologic Museum in the mid-1990s.

By this time in cryptologic history, communications, computers, and cryptography had developed to a level that permitted the incorporation of all three functions into one piece of equipment.

A good example of such integration is the MISTE II. This suitcase-size piece of military equipment is a complete satellite communications terminal that can handle several types of data and has an integrated encryption/decryption function. A variety of similar commercial equipment were entering the marketplace in this general time frame as well.

## Late 1980s

The Internet was opened to commercial use as commercial e-mail providers were authorized to use the National Science Foundation Network (NSFNET) backbone.

Two privately funded companies, UUNet and Performance Systems International (PSI), were spun off from government programs.

As access to networks expanded and bandwidth increased, new applications appeared. Voice was no longer the dominant information on networks as many types of digital data joined analog video transmissions. The term "multimedia applications" came into use along with requirements to be able to mix data types while being able to use transmission paths in an economical manner. A variety of network architectures evolved. The International Telecommunication Union (ITU) continued to develop Broadband Integrated Services Digital Network (BISDN) standards. These standards addressed an ever-growing need for high-speed digital interconnections for streaming Internet applications as well as digital, video, and imagery. Requirements emerged for a service to economically support variable data rate traffic or bandwidth on demand. Asynchronous Transfer Mode (ATM) was one of the standards aimed at supporting the growing data transfer needs within the BISDN structure. ATM combines techniques of fast-packet switching and data-multiplexing techniques. ATM transfers information in fixed-size units called *cells*. Each cell is of fixed length and contains both cell-header information and the payload (user information). The relatively small fixed-length cells are well suited to transferring voice and video traffic because such traffic is intolerant of delays that result from having to wait for large data packet transfers.

ATM's advantage is that it statistically prevents wasted network capacity. When users request service, the network determines both the users' average and peak bandwidth and priority requirements. Knowing average and peak load requirements of other competing users, the network controller makes an automatic determination, on a statistical basis, whether sufficient switching and multiplexing capacity is available to support the requested service. With ATM, usable capacity was dynamically assigned. Networks were becoming "smart."

## 1988

The first transatlantic (United States to United Kingdom) fiber-optic cable was put into service by AT&T (TAT-8).

## 1989

Clifford Stoll published *The Cuckoo's Egg*, and the public was introduced to the dangers of the Internet hacker.

## Early 1990s

The availability of freeware, shareware, and commercial software products online and in stores reduced the time, cost, and difficulty of building applications. Non-experts built Web sites, and hackers became a worldwide menace.

As mentioned previously, both large- and small-scale computers and their applications developed rapidly. Although it was advantageous both to the cryptographer and to cryptanalysis to have access to the most advanced computing tools available, most of the cryptologic advancements in the last decade have focused on software implementations of advanced mathematical concepts. Their details remain classified for obvious reasons.

Cryptographers have also had to respond to the telecommunications requirements of the times, such as the wide application of ATM switching. ATM has many modes, but all integrate both multiplexing and switching functions. In some of the most useful applications, ATM equipment serves communications paths that have defined end points, but the bandwidth available on the routes is allocated according to the demands of the traffic being transmitted. A new generation of cryptographic techniques had to be developed to match this networking concept.

One response to the ATM capability was the KG-75 series of equipments. These equipments can handle data rates in excess of 600 Mbps and generate cryptographic keys in a dynamic manner for each connection. They can also handle a wide variety of data including those generated by multiuser computer groups. They can operate in a variety of network configurations in both simplex and duplex modes. They can use either manual or remote rekeying. These devices use modern VLSI electronics, weigh less than forty pounds, and consume less than 100 watts of power. They provide a clear example of a development in cryptographic equipment responding to the challenges of advanced communications systems.

## 1990

Microsoft introduced Windows 3.0, the first usable version of its answer to Apple's graphical user interface.

## 1991

Linus Torvalds, a student at Helsinki University, introduced LINUX, an operating system based on UNIX, for the PC and offered it free of charge.

Tim Berners-Lee at the European Organization for Nuclear Research (CERN) released the World Wide Web architecture.

The first digital cellular systems were installed in the United States.

## 1992

The number of Internet hosts exceeded one million.

A typical cellular phone relay antenna tower. This suburban antenna installation is a
good example of the thousands of similar towers around the United States. Although the
phones themselves may be small and inconspicuous, the antenna systems that support
their use are not.

## 1993

An international coordinating body responsible for technical and operational issues associated with telecommunications was formed from the CCITT. It was made a part of the ITU and called the ITU Telecommunications Standardization Sector (ITU-T). It was the then-current international administrative body that promotes standards and practices in more than twenty technical areas.

## 1994

The first satellite of the MILSTAR joint service satellite communications system was launched on February 7. This advanced geostationary system would provide secure, jam-resistant communications to all military users. Rather than being a single-hop relay system, each MILSTAR satellite serves as a switchboard and processes the signals on board, relaying them as required through satellite-to-

MILSTAR, a switchboard in the sky. The multisatellite geosynchronous communications system provides secure, jam-resistant, worldwide service to all military services. Each satellite weighs about ten thousand pounds on orbit and the solar arrays generate about 8,000 watts of power. *U.S. Air Force*

satellite communications crosslinks. The prime contractor for the system was the Lockheed Martin Missiles and Space Company. TRW Inc. was the payload contractor. The Air Force Space and Missile Systems Center was responsible for the development and acquisition of the program.

In the civilian sector, the number of cellular telephone users was estimated to be about sixteen million in the United States. (Growth continued at about 50 percent per year, similar to growth rates of the telephone, automobile, and television in the United States after their first introductions.)

James Gosling of Sun Microsystems invented the Java programming language, which permitted programmers to write software for any computer operating system on the Internet.

## 1997

The number of World Wide Web sites exceeded one million.

## 1999

The number of cellular telephone users in the world was estimated to be about 470 million.

## 2000

Although the early 2000s saw considerable business turmoil in the high-tech communications sector, few of the problems were caused by technological factors. The uses of advanced communications techniques continued to spread aggressively worldwide.

A Compaq high-capacity system using seven hundred interconnected 64-bit processors, capable of 1.3 trillion floating point operations per second (1.3 TeraOps), and coupled to a 50-terabyte database was used by Celera Genomics to provide the first blueprint of the human genome. Although the laptop computer had taken over many functions, a continuing need for large computational complexes and specialized computer architectures remained. New computer architectures and new technologies to implement them were being developed every day all over the world.

## 2001

The U.S. Department of Energy's Accelerated Strategic Computing Initiative (ACSI) produced the next-generation supercomputer as the Lawrence Livermore National Laboratory put a 12.3 TeraOps supercomputer, called ACSI White, into operation. Its intended use was to investigate highly complex simulation prob-

Celera supercomputing facility, circa 2001. This complex, one of the most powerful civilian supercomputing facilities in the world, was first used to map the human genome. As shown in this wide-angle photograph, it provides 1.3 teraflops of computing power derived from a distributed set of 1,200 Compaq Alpha processors and eight specialized computers designed by Paracel. The complex has access to 80 terabytes of storage. Approximately two hundred miles of optical fiber are used for the high-speed interconnections. *Celera Genomics*

lems such as fusion explosions and earthquake analysis. The machine was designed and produced by IBM and contains 8,192 microprocessors that are arranged into clusters. The clusters communicate at up to 4 Gb/s through a crossbar switch. There are 4 terabytes of RAM, 10 terabytes of rapid-access disk, and 150 terabytes of global disk memory. This very large computer occupies more than twenty thousand square feet of floor space and requires a dedicated 10.35 Mwatt power station.

The next step was planned to be "ACSI Q," which would operate at more than 30 TeraOps and would initially consist of more than twelve thousand processors, each running at 1250 MHz and having access to more than 600 terabytes of memory. The contract was awarded late in 2000 to Compaq.

Supercomputers continued to press for performance, but they were not alone. This year the world microprocessor market was estimated to be worth about $40 billion.

Intelsat, responding to the dynamics of the worldwide telecommunications marketplace, became a public corporation in July and announced the intent to sell 15 percent of its shares to the public within a year.

Estimates put the number of Internet users worldwide at more than 400 million. Up to 60 percent of the U.S. population was thought to use the Internet.

# 2002

Advances continued in all areas, and some proved to be revolutionary. For example, a Swiss company that was an offshoot of the University of Geneva, id Quantique, introduced two new products based on the principles of quantum computing. One of these products was a random-number generator and the second was a method of solving the problem of cryptographic key exchange. Again, cryptographers were at the leading edges of new technologies.[12]

Hewlett-Packard bought Compaq in a much-debated major acquisition.

Late in the year, the Nippon Electric Co., Ltd. (NEC), announced that it had placed its new Earth Simulator supercomputer into operation at the nation's Earth Simulator Center. This computer used 5,120 networked processors and operated at almost 41 TeraOps. This was the first time Japan had laid claim to the "world's fastest" title.

IBM announced that it would deliver a pair of supercomputers to the U.S. Department of Energy that would be three times as fast as the NEC system.

As applications expanded and business grew around the world, computer developments continued. From microcomputer to supercomputer, computing was a dynamic field. Even the adjectives that describe the most powerful of the powerful were being replaced—the term *supercomputer* changed to hypercomputer. Many scientific problems required these always-expensive tools, including climate modeling, controlled fusion, medicine and biosciences, weapons testing, astronomy, and, yes, cryptology.

The continuing expansion of secure communications capability within both government and industry improved operational potential at all organizational levels and facilitated widespread use of the Internet for private purposes in ways that would have been difficult to image even only forty years ago.

More than forty years of progress since World War II have brought many changes to the technical, operational, and management aspects of cryptology.

In chapter 6 we characterized the application of cryptographic devices at the end of World War II by the following features:

They were government developed and produced.

They used secret government algorithms.

They were implemented in separate subsystems (i.e., "boxes" with government nomenclatures) and treated as classified material.

They were installed, operated, and controlled by government authorities in designated facilities or as parts of military units.

They required physical contact for keying.

Today, the story is much different:

Many advances in and uses for cryptography extend beyond the government, although the U.S. government is still an active player in the field.

Many algorithms are available not only to the public, but also for export.

Some government subsystems are treated as unclassified when they are not keyed, and a strong trend is emerging toward integrating security functions into the systems that they serve.

The public sector widely uses encryption devices to support many types of activities (financial, medical, law enforcement, and others).

Several kinds of remote keying are used in both commercial and government applications.

A good illustration of the technological progress since World War II can be seen when comparing the SIGSALY voice-security equipment with today's STU-III. SIGSALY, a technological marvel for its time, weighed more than fifty tons, required a dedicated special radio system, provided marginal voice quality, required an extensive logistics system to supply the cryptographic key, and was very expensive. For all these reasons, it was available at only the highest levels of government. The STU-III is economical, available to hundreds of thousands of users, is about the size of an average telephone desk set, and can be used world-wide over many types of regular telephone networks. No market exists today for a several-hundred-pound telephone, much less a fifty-ton one. Nevertheless, many bright and dedicated government and industry employees joined together to cre-ate a sustained technology "push" and requirements "pull" to forge remarkable progress in a relatively brief period.

Legitimate national security concerns make it difficult to provide a current example of changes in cryptanalytic-tool technology, but we can logically assume that the most advanced computer, software, and mathematical capabilities are being applied, just as they have been in the past. Today's laptop computers are as powerful as the supercomputers of the past, yet markets are emerging for even faster and more powerful hypercomputers.

Today's challenges may differ from those we faced more than forty years ago, but the available tools for attacking the problems have also advanced significantly.

Standing still is not an option—it never has been!

# 8

# SUMMARY

Over time, combined advances in the three technology fields of this history—communications, computers, and cryptology—formed an intense drama. Individuals, universities, industries, and governments all have major roles, and their interactions and developments produce significant and, often unintended, consequences.

We have seen the many ways that the technological developments in communications, computers, and cryptography are intertwined. The interrelationships are technically complex, as are the driving forces for both the developments and their applications. Although military applications often drove progress, industrial market pressures have at times pulled the military and government applications along with them. Governmental policies on import, export, and business practices have had some impact on development, but more often commercial applications have been the driving force. However, governmental support of key activities is crucial to this story and should not be understated. In all cases, brilliant and determined key individuals have driven progress.

The following examples illustrate the subtle yet complex nature of the interrelationships. They have been mentioned earlier, and we will expand on them here.

Marconi's invention of the radio and its quick acceptance by a broad variety of markets made clear to many users the need for advances in cryptographic capability.

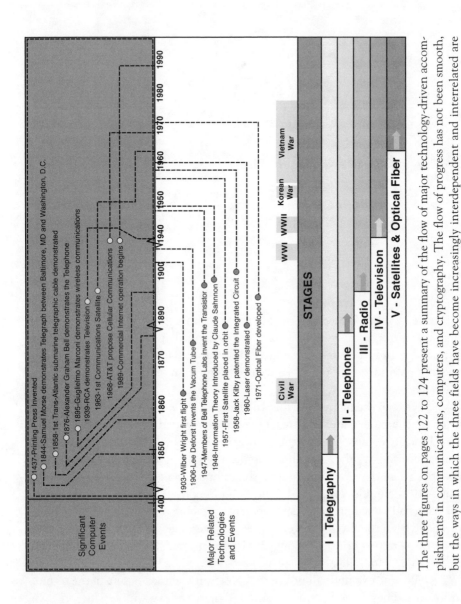

The three figures on pages 122 to 124 present a summary of the flow of major technology-driven accomplishments in communications, computers, and cryptography. The flow of progress has not been smooth, but the ways in which the three fields have become increasingly interdependent and interrelated are important to recognize. *R.E. Conley*

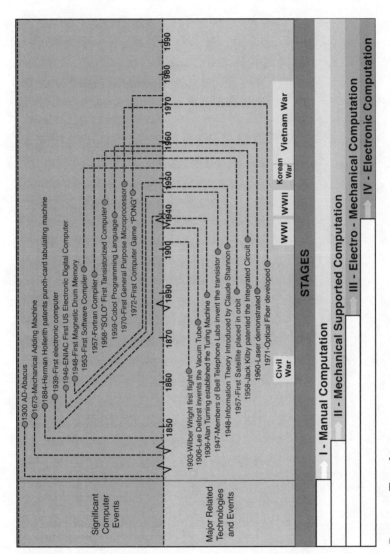

Computer Time Line

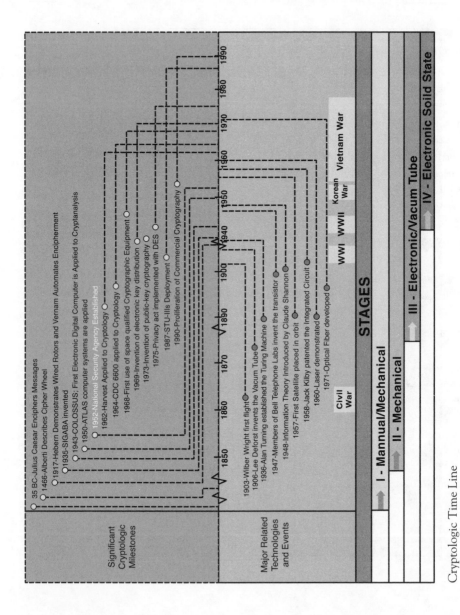

Cryptologic Time Line

The telegraph was the tool that demonstrated the clear advantages of communicating rapidly over long distances. We have mentioned the rapid acceptance of this tool in military affairs, as demonstrated in the U.S. Civil War. Cryptographic tools, though primitive, were in widespread use. Both Union and Confederate intelligence units engaged in what would now be called "information warfare." Each devoted resources to reading the other side's secret communications, took inventive action to intercept the opponent's messages, and used deceptive information to promote military operations.[1]

The use of radio meant that communicators no longer needed physical connections with each other. Radio was quickly accommodated into all activities, both civilian and military, that could benefit from rapid long-distance communication. For example, only about six years after Marconi's first demonstration in 1895, the U.S. Navy had experimented with ship-to-shore radio and only five years later had equipped more than fifty ships with radio for regular use. The Navy was now able to quickly coordinate actions and activities over distances of thousands of miles.

Rapid progress continued, evidenced by the first air-to-ground radio transmission, which occurred only seven years after the Wright brothers' first airplane flight in 1903. Business management uses of radio messages also became popular.

As uses of radio spread, it became obvious long-ranged "broadcast" could have a built-in disadvantage: anyone could listen with relative ease. Ensuring privacy required the special precautions that cryptography provided. However, what was once acceptable for written messages and even telegraphic transmissions was now viewed as a distinct drawback; that is, cryptography had been tailored to the needs of written transmission and therefore new technology for radio needed to be developed. These developments were pursued in the private sector and with government resources. It was some time before the technology of cryptography was mechanized to a point that it could be used with relative convenience for radio.

World War II hastened developments in all three fields. In particular, the use of new digital communications techniques and the development of computational capability were closely associated with cryptography.

The electromechanical devices that were being used in communications, computational applications, and cryptography in the late 1930s were great advances over the technologies in use just a decade or so earlier. However, two main problems remained:

1. No satisfactory means of securing voice communications was available.
2. The most advanced electromechanical encryption machines for transmitting data presented cryptanalytic challenges that could be met only with much faster computational capability.

Electronic vacuum-tube technology was available. Engineering and manufacturing skills had been developed to support wide use of this technology. Ingenious people who recognized the importance of the success of their work applied themselves and, just as important, gained the support of their governments for the allocation of the required resources. Their results were systems such as SIGSALY in the United States (first secure digital voice system) and COLOSSUS (arguably the first large-scale digital computer) in the United Kingdom.

Of course, not all technical advances were directly related to cryptography. The recognized priorities of this time period drove many other important advances, including radio direction finding, microwave multichannel communications systems, and practical radar systems. Army-sponsored computer work at the University of Pennsylvania (mentioned in chapter 5) produced ENIAC, an important contribution to computer development. In the postwar period, many individuals who had worked in one field or the other began to take their knowledge to other areas. Progress thus continued at a rapid pace after the war.

Claude Shannon's *A Mathematical Theory of Communications* and his subsequent work, *Communication Theory of Secrecy Systems*, were surely provoked by his wartime activities.[2] Concerning developments in the three fields of our primary interest, Shannon's works and Alan Turing's *On Computable Numbers* may have had the greatest impact on subsequent public developments, although John von Neumann's *First Draft of a Report on EDVAC* was also important.

The point is that the events of World War II energized both theoretical and engineering accomplishments, which accelerated progress in communications, computers, and cryptology. The applications of these accomplishments (and, of course, progress in many other areas of technology) were positive forces in the Allied wartime efforts.

Urgent national priorities will no doubt prompt further technological innovation, but one hopes that war will not always be the factor that provokes the attention. We have an obvious need for a wide-based understanding of the potential of technology to solve problems. This understanding will be fully realized only when a larger proportion of the general population is educated in the basics of sciences and engineering.

Governmental use of national secrecy rules and an active government marketplace affected the evolution of all three fields. The computer industry is a particularly good example.

Technologies that are developed and applied for wartime use are often subject to classification and export/import restrictions. While these limitations restrict the flow of knowledge (indeed, that is their primary purpose), they may also have far-reaching, unintended consequences. Of course, we cannot place ourselves in the pressure-filled circumstances at the end of World War II and the code-breaking activities at Bletchley Park. However, we can speculate as to what might have happened as the worldwide computer industry developed if the British had not made the severe decision to destroy COLOSSUS and all of the related materials at the end of the war.

In the late 1940s, the United Kingdom was the site of significant computer developments at both Manchester University (the first stored program computer) and Cambridge University. Alan Turing, continuing his work on his ideas at the National Physical Laboratory, was one of the first to explore the field of artificial intelligence. Although the computer field had some industrial involvement in the United Kingdom, a sizeable computer industry in the United States grew quickly, driven by the following factors: the unclassified presentations of von Neumann's EDVAC report, subsequent public workshops on the topic at the University of Pennsylvania, and courses at several other universities (MIT and Princeton in particular), along with the business goals of Eckert, Mauchly, Norris, and others (some with cryptologic experience).[3]

Who knows what would have happened if the EDVAC report and the associated work had been classified—or if the work on COLOSSUS had continued. A different speculative story is that of SIGSALY, the secure digital voice system developed by BTL. The specifics of this system, though not destroyed, did remain classified for a very long time (more than thirty years). In addition, the government continued to support classified work on the ciphony techniques at BTL and other institutions, and BTL was free to apply much of the basic technology "firsts" to other public applications. In this case, although the duration of the classification may have been unnecessarily long, advances in digital communications did proceed. Would advancement have been more rapid under less severe classification restrictions? We will never know.

We do know that relatively rapid declassification of other technologies related to multichannel microwave systems (and radar) led to rapid expansion of high-capacity telephone systems and many other marketplaces.

In the case of public-key cryptography, the public sector developed and applied the technology not only without the help of classified government research, but also over the opposition of governmental authorities. Clearly, classification and export restrictions are serious factors affecting advanced technologies, the state of a nation's technical business base, and other national security factors.

Public debate has ensued over these secrecy and export points concerning cryptography. These debates have sometimes been distracting and other times helpful. Debaters still disagree as to which is which. While few would deny that advanced cryptographic techniques play an important role in national security, many still disagree about the degree to which national security considerations should be allowed to impact legitimate business interests. Although no fixed answer to this dilemma has been forthcoming, at least the last few years have seen the debate proceed on an informed basis.

The advent of space-borne communications systems enabled true worldwide communications services. The use of geosynchronous satellite platforms for communications relay purposes provided a reliable and cost-effective method of communicating over long distances. This situation was predicted by Arthur C. Clarke in 1945 while he was still on active duty as a radar officer with the Royal Air Force.[4] He was well into his science fiction writing career before the technologies became available that fulfilled his prediction. The first satellite was not flown until 1957, and the first geosynchronous system was not put into operation until 1963. Perhaps no better example has emerged of how good ideas can quickly transfer between disciplines. Several government agencies, along with the aerospace and communications industries, worked together in complex ways to quickly establish the capability to use geosynchronous communications satellite systems. Their uses have become widespread in many areas from intelligence applications to home entertainment. They provide communications and data services to a wide variety of customers ranging from military command and control authorities to missionary outposts in some of the most remote regions of the world.

Not all aspects of Clarke's predictions were correct. He predicted the potential of space-relay to be so vast that ground-based relay systems would become obsolete. Such obsolescence has not occurred because these systems continue to provide economical service and because they have been integrated into long-haul networks that employ high-capacity fiber-optic cables (a development that Clarke, like many others, did not foresee). What we now have is an ever-expanding complex of communications options that system designers can employ for many purposes.

Cryptography is an integral part of most communications systems and the information they carry. Some systems use it only to protect the command and control functions of the satellite systems themselves, while others depend on elaborate cryptographic systems to protect the information channels. In like manner, computer technology is imbedded in every segment of the system operation whether its intended use is military or civilian.

This type of expanding system is a great example of how communications, computers, and cryptology (of course, along with several other technologies) are required to advance simultaneously in order to improve the basic service provided to users. It is widely recognized today that for networked communications capability to further develop and successfully expand, it must depend on all three basic technologies.

Only a few visionaries may have appreciated the predictions of Arthur C. Clarke, but most current practitioners in any of our primary fields intuitively understand that to forge advances in the capability of any one of these fields they must consider the state-of-the-art in all of them.

Today's advanced high-capacity computer systems are a good example of the need for this understanding. At some scale, the modern supercomputer can be viewed as a set of data processors and memory subsystems linked together by a complex high-capacity, high-speed communications network. Cryptography protects files within the system, authenticates access to parts of a trusted system, and ensures the integrity of information transmitted outside of the computer system itself. Growth potential still exists with today's technologies. New developments will drive new applications and, in turn, new markets and applications will forge technology developments in all three fields.

A healthy international marketplace continues to be a driving force for development in all three fields. The above statement may be self-evident, but it expresses a fact that policymakers and the business sector have sometimes ignored. The saga of public key cryptography provides a relevant example although it is perhaps somewhat of a chicken-and-egg story. In the absence of worldwide communications networks, the many related public uses of those networks, and the computer capacity to both support the networks themselves and drive the range of applications, a large demand for the public key cryptographic technologies may never have emerged. And vice versa. The worlds of trade policy, patent law, banking, equity markets, international business agreements, and, yes, intelligence activities are all tightly connected to international marketplace issues. As worldwide concern rises about the influence of international trade organizations, those working in high-technology fields (particularly the three we have been discussing) must stay abreast of these developments to gain the support required for new advances.

New technological developments often have unexpected, sometimes negative, consequences. The former director of the policy planning staff of the U.S. Department of State, Ambassador Richard N. Haass, has recently observed: "The revolution in information and communications technologies has helped integrate the world and its economies as never before. While helping accelerate the economic dynamism of the past decade, these same technologies facilitate the coordination of transnational criminal and terrorist networks. Other technologies also have their own bright and dark sides."[5]

Although the marketplace is a major factor in the acceptance of advances in technology, history reveals that the marketplace rarely calls out for these new advances. It is a topic that is difficult to handle at the level of a single company; we should not be surprised that it is almost impossible to manage at a national level. Technological advancement is often (not always) associated with business innovation. Some universities, MIT being an outstanding example, have combined

their engineering and technological activities with business and innovation principles to give their students a head start in the business world. Innovation, now
the subject of scholarly work, will affect the work of technologists whether or not
they realize it.[6]

Overall progress has been brought about by the contributions of individuals in
many fields. Although their motivations and backgrounds varied, progress would
have been much slower at best without their personal contributions.

Advances in mathematics, physics, and engineering have often inspired those
who have forged advances in technology in our three fields. However, we have
emphasized that key insights and energy come from others who may not be
involved full-time in technology; examples include Samuel F. B. Morse, portrait
painter; Arthur C. Clarke, fledgling science fiction writer; and, earlier, Johannes
Tritemius, Benedictine abbot. Industry, government, and universities all produced the people who made the essential contributions. It is a complex and interacting process that resists simplification or prediction.

Our story highlights those individuals who have achieved success and recognition. Many others tried and failed, nearly had success, or exhausted their
resources just before they tasted success. In some cases, the competition for fame,
patent rights, and marketing advantage dragged on for years. In other cases, some
major players were ignored for one reason or another, and their contributions
were recognized much later. Creating and applying leading-edge technology is an
active, energetic process with many participants. All of them are important, yet
we usually see only the winners.

Support for activities that advance technology is obtained from government,
industry, and university sources. Government funding has significantly influenced technology developments in all three fields. The creation of the Internet is
an excellent example. Although no specific government goal for creating the
Internet existed, and someday a similar development would have arguably
emerged without government support, the related Defense Advanced Research
Projects Agency (DARPA) and NSF programs played an extremely important
role. The computer industry is another obvious example. Robert Seidel succinctly
describes this case: "As the midwife for the computing industry, the government
made it possible to emerge from the womb of war to the world of peace."[7]

Although government support is clearly important, the dynamics of the technology, along with other factors, make it very difficult (probably impossible) to
plan the process of technological development in detail whether the planner
works in government, industry, or academia. Periodic efforts are made to access
the status of an area and produce guidance and recommendations. They are useful exercises. John Hendry has examined the evolution of the British computer
industry in some detail in his work *Innovating for Failure: Government Policy and*

*the Early British Computer Industry*. As the title suggests, he contrasts post–World War II events in the United States and Great Britain, particularly as they relate to Britain's National Research Development Corporation (NRDC) and the difficulty of exploiting Britain's technological capability in electronic computing because of its successful cryptologic activities. His work illustrates the complexity of any high-level planning process involving technology. At one point he notes that consensus is usually a prerequisite for decisions on government sponsorship, particularly at high levels. He then observes, "Unfortunately, in the world of new and complex technologies, technical consensus is quite simply an impossibility."[8]

Determining the actual levels of government sponsorship for a given technology area is difficult, but most will probably agree that it is still worth trying. One good example of the 1990s noted the U.S. Department of Defense as the largest source of federal research support in computer science and engineering,[9] followed by NSF, NASA, and the U.S. Department of Energy. Meaningful data across all three interacting fields are difficult to obtain, but efforts continue to periodically measure the resources being applied. In our economy, few would voluntarily judge the appropriateness of the resources, but policymakers in each area continue to benchmark trends.

The joy of working in one of the three dynamic fields of communications, computers, and cryptology is that no one can really predict what the future will hold. A popular quote from Arthur C. Clarke is "Any sufficiently advanced technology is indistinguishable from magic."

Gaining support for a new technology program requires imagination, whether one presents a proposal in a bureaucratic planning meeting, a faculty working session, a meeting with investment bankers, or to one's spouse. Those who stand a chance of succeeding must understand the force behind the "magic" and somehow acquire the resources. To get ahead, faster is better, but success often takes a long time.

Today the three fields of communications, computers, and cryptology are more closely related than at any other time in history. Recognizing their interdependence may be the key to further advancements.

We began this book by noting that Americans experience the interactions of communications, computers, and cryptography daily. We trust that we have illustrated this fact, which less than fifty years ago was not well recognized. The evolution of cryptographic equipment in the military marketplace shows the interactions and growth of technology in all three areas.

As we have noted, the cryptographic functions of the military communicator became integrated with data transmission only in the 1940s. Postwar communications and data security equipments were specially designed subsystems that were physically external from the basic communications equipment. Soon, advances in technology allowed the security equipment to be integrated into the basic equipment itself, usually in the form of an integrated circuit board or sub-assembly. As the complexity of integrated electronics increased, all manner of functions could be accommodated as software functions. This path has led to the point at which many cryptographic functions are now completely integrated into communications system designs; they have become software functions in a multi-purpose computer environment. The home computer that supports Internet operations is an example of how commercial products have evolved.

Technological factors alone neither create the changes nor force the interactions among the three fields. Many have commented on this fact. Thomas L. Friedman clearly and concisely describes the overall situation:

> To begin with the Cold War system was characterized by one overarching feature—division. The world was a divided-up, chopped-up place and both your threats and opportunities in the Cold War system tended to grow out of whom you were divided from. Appropriately, the Cold War system was symbolized by a single word: the *wall*—the Berlin Wall . . .
>
> The globalization system is a bit different. It also has one overarching feature—integration. The world has become an increasingly interwoven place, and today, whether you are a company or a country, your threats and opportunities derive from who you are connected to. This globalization system is also characterized by a single word: the *Web*.[10]

The technologies of communications, computers, and cryptology have all interacted in ways that brought about these important global changes, and they have provided support for our activities within the new and evolving structures. They will no doubt help to construct whatever comes next. All three technology areas are important building blocks for the future.

As new systems of all sorts are conceptualized, today's system engineers have the capability to make performance trades that involve all three fields. This capability will open up new and different system architectures in many systems and will permit some new system concepts to be implemented. Which ones will catch on? It remains to be seen.

Predicting what is "next" in any of these fields is a practical impossibility. The only clear prediction: changes *will* come and the nation that enjoys leading-edge status in all three technologies stands to make significant gains. Military command, control, and intelligence activities are obvious beneficiaries of a leading-edge strategy.

# Appendix A

## INTRODUCTION TO CRYPTOLOGY

### Cryptology?

As noted in chapter 1, the term *cryptography* is generally referred to as the science and study of secret writing; when we use the term, we are describing the arts and sciences of securing information by encryption. Likewise, we use "cryptanalysis" to mean the arts and sciences used by unintended recipients for recovering plaintext from ciphertext. Both aspects of the problem are combined in the term *cryptology*, which, at least in our definition, includes all of the activities that are conducted to both protect and exploit information of any type, whether in transit, in storage, or in processing.

The science of cryptology is quite old. When a significant number of people had learned to communicate by means of the written word, they realized the need to keep some information secret from the general population. The birthdate is not exactly clear, perhaps as early as 1900 BC, but cryptology was soon born.[1] Still alive, well, and developing, it has, over its lifetime, taken on an elegant mathematical personality, along with the attributes of engineering and technology that we describe in this book. It is a fascinating subject for many reasons.

One reason for this fascination is the general aura of secrecy associated with intelligence activities. After all, if the object is to keep the information secret, why would anyone volunteer to explain how the process works? Of course, the intended recipient of the information must be able to decrypt the material easily.

But why would a professional cryptographer challenge his counterparts in public? Naturally, there are many good reasons to share information. Teaching is one. We have also seen that the growth and utility of modern communications and computer systems have, as a by-product, encouraged new cryptographic techniques. Without going into any technical detail at all, it is logical (and correct) to assume that the cryptographic systems of today are complex in their fundamental mathematics and their use of advanced technology. They are also "secure" because of that situation. How secure is "secure"? It depends on many factors, including the skill and resources of those who would like to know the content of the communication. The tension is naturally strong between the cryptographer and the cryptanalyst.

Dr. Abrahm Sinkov, one of the World War II pioneers in cryptology,[2] makes this observation about cryptanalysis: "The analytical processes used by a cryptanalyst require a number of techniques: some mathematical, some linguistic, some of an engineering character, and some not readily describable such as luck, flair, sixth sense, etc."[3]

Indeed, all of these techniques and traits are still in demand today. They are always in short supply, yet the level of difficulty of the problems presented by cryptanalysis continues to attract the very best talent. In this book we focus primarily on technology (those attributes that Dr. Sinkov would say involved processes of "engineering character"). Without the creative talents of the people involved in the cryptologic arts and sciences, however, there can be no national leadership in the field among nations.

The process of maintaining a position of national leadership is a very complex one, but a general understanding of the topic can be acquired fairly easily. Today's technical literature, both professional and recreational, provides many starting points for a further, more complete understanding of cryptology. What follows here is an introduction only; references are provided for a further detail and follow-up.

## What Is a Code, and What Is a Cipher?

Unfortunately, the two terms *code* and *cipher* are often used interchangeably. In a philosophical sense, all ciphers are codes, but not all codes are ciphers. But this explanation may not help the reader develop an intuitive sense of which is which. Does it really matter? That is a good question. The answer is yes, sometimes.

It is helpful to think of a code as a means of representing something (a letter, a word, a function, a numeral, or something more complex such as a name or a command) by something else that may or may not be of the same form. Codebooks may be thought of as something like a dictionary that is used to convert plain language into a different (often secret) language. The Morse code, mentioned in chapter 3, used letters and numerals to transmit dots and dashes. Without knowing the code, the symbols would be meaningless (but fairly easy to figure out). Otherwise, they are intended to be clearly understood.

Many other examples of everyday codes exist. One is the Baudot code (see chapter 3), which was intended for the mechanization of teletype. There are

| Binary | LTRS | FIGS |
|--------|------|------|
| 00011  | A    | –    |
| 11001  | B    | ?    |
| 01110  | C    | :    |
| 01001  | D    | $    |
| 00001  | E    | 3    |
| 01101  | F    | !    |
| 11010  | G    | &    |
| 10100  | H    | #    |
| 00110  | I    | 8    |
| 01011  | J    | BELL |
| 01111  | K    | (    |
| 10010  | L    | )    |
| 11100  | M    | .    |
| 01100  | N    | ,    |
| 11000  | O    | 9    |
| 10110  | P    | 0    |
| 10111  | Q    | 1    |
| 01010  | R    | 4    |
| 00101  | S    | '    |
| 10000  | T    | 5    |
| 00111  | U    | 7    |
| 11110  | V    | ;    |
| 10011  | W    | 2    |
| 11101  | X    | /    |
| 10101  | Y    | 6    |
| 10001  | Z    | "    |
| 01000  | CR   | CR   |
| 00010  | LF   | LF   |
| 00100  | SP   | SP   |
| 11111  | LTRS | LTRS |
| 11011  | FIGS | FIGS |
| 00000  | [..unused..] | |

Baudot uses two code subsets, the "letter set" (LTRS), and the "figure set" (FIGS). The FIGS character (11011) signals that the following code is to be interpreted as being in the FIGS set, until this is reset by the LTRS (11111) character.

**5 Bits**

0 1 0 0 1

Amplitude

**Time**

The above 5 bits in time describe the letter "D" in the Baudot Code

Representation of the Baudot teletype code. The Baudot code developed in 1870 was a binary representation. The Baudot code was represented as either a mark (1) or a space (0) and translated into equal time intervals as the electrical current "on" and electric current "off" for transmission. Five bits represented a letter (twenty-six uppercase letters of the alphabet) or figures that included numerals 0 through 9 plus symbols for a carriage return and ringing a bell on the teletype machine, alerting the operator. Variants of the Baudot code and the teletype machine were in common use in World War I.

many international standards for data transmission today, as well as many unique codes. Some are quite complex and incorporate features such as "error correction," which enables the sending and receiving ends of a transmission to automatically limit the number of transmission errors contained in the received data. Today, all manner of data are encoded, including text, speech, photographic images, graphics material, and measurement information. The cryptologic skill called "signals analysis" is primarily involved with determining the structure and application of such codes.

Although the primary purpose of this type of code is to preserve data, rather than protect the information from unauthorized access, it is also true that the term "codes" includes the use of words, terms, or data sets that may be unintelligible to unauthorized recipients simply because they do not have the equivalent of the dictionary (or codebook). In such situations, cryptanalytic skills, combined with signal analysis, are frequently useful.

Code wheel

A cipher is the result of a process that is intended to protect the meaning of the communication (or data, whether transmitted or stored) from unauthorized access. The process of encipherment may be simple or complex. Complexity alone does not always ensure success, and the cryptanalyst is likely to refer to encipherment as either "strong" or "weak," which are terms directly related to the assumed cryptanalytic capability; they do not reflect any absolute measurement. One cipher may be "strong" for one adversary and "weak" for another. About the only absolute in this profession is that successful cryptanalysts are, by nature, very tight-lipped! They live in a fragile world where they must work hard for any advantage.

The cryptographer has the natural advantage, as the following simple example will demonstrate. This simple example of a substitution cipher, where each letter of the original plaintext is replaced by another letter in a predetermined manner, is sometimes called the Caesar cipher as it was known to be used during the time of Julius Caesar. Note the similarity to the cipher disk of Alberti, described in chapter 2. In this example, the two alphabets are offset by three letters as indicated by the arrow. This offset, three, is the "key" to the substitution. With the plain text of A set on the inner ring, the ciphertext would be D as shown on the outer ring. Even a simple message such as ATTACK AT DAWN takes on a strange look as follows:

Plaintext:    A T T A C K A T D A W N
Cipher text: D W W D F N D W G D Z Q

If the cryptanalyst wanted to simply search for the key by trying all of the twenty-five possible offsets in some sequence, it might take twenty-five tries, or it might be found on the first try. Note that there are some other characteristics in the ciphertext (repeated letters and combinations) that could be exploited. The cryptanalyst would note the use of double letters, the short words, etc., and would use knowledge of the rules of spelling, statistics on the use of letters in the language, and other linguistic features in the analysis. The longer the message, the more useful these facts would be. In fact, this simple substitution cipher would not be judged to be "strong" to anyone with even a rudimentary knowledge of the language in use. However, even in this simple example, it should be obvious that the cryptanalytic process is very likely to require significantly more effort than the cryptographic process did in the first place.

A contribution of Blaise de Vigenère (see chapter 2) can provide an illustration of how cryptographers complicate the lives of cryptanalysts. Communicators would start with the simple tableau shown below, noting that the rows are each a Caesar cipher with increasing offsets.

The communicators would also create a shared (and secret) keyword. For this example, the keyword will be CRYPTOLOGY. The previous example message,

```
  A B C D E F G H I J K L M N O P Q R S T U V W X Y Z

A A B C D E F G H I J K L M N O P Q R S T U V W X Y Z
B B C D E F G H I J K L M N O P Q R S T U V W X Y Z A
C C D E F G H I J K L M N O P Q R S T U V W X Y Z A B
D D E F G H I J K L M N O P Q R S T U V W X Y Z A B C
E E F G H I J K L M N O P Q R S T U V W X Y Z A B C D
F F G H I J K L M N O P Q R S T U V W X Y Z A B C D E
G G H I J K L M N O P Q R S T U V W X Y Z A B C D E F
H H I J K L M N O P Q R S T U V W X Y Z A B C D E F G
I I J K L M N O P Q R S T U V W X Y Z A B C D E F G H
J J K L M N O P Q R S T U V W X Y Z A B C D E F G H I
K K L M N O P Q R S T U V W X Y Z A B C D E F G H I J
L L M N O P Q R S T U V W X Y Z A B C D E F G H I J K
M M N O P Q R S T U V W X Y Z A B C D E F G H I J K L
N N O P Q R S T U V W X Y Z A B C D E F G H I J K L M
O O P Q R S T U V W X Y Z A B C D E F G H I J K L M N
P P Q R S T U V W X Y Z A B C D E F G H I J K L M N O
Q Q R S T U V W X Y Z A B C D E F G H I J K L M N O P
R R S T U V W X Y Z A B C D E F G H I J K L M N O P Q
S S T U V W X Y Z A B C D E F G H I J K L M N O P Q R
T T U V W X Y Z A B C D E F G H I J K L M N O P Q R S
U U V W X Y Z A B C D E F G H I J K L M N O P Q R S T
V V W X Y Z A B C D E F G H I J K L M N O P Q R S T U
W W X Y Z A B C D E F G H I J K L M N O P Q R S T U V
X X Y Z A B C D E F G H I J K L M N O P Q R S T U V W
Y Y Z A B C D E F G H I J K L M N O P Q R S T U V W X
Z Z A B C D E F G H I J K L M N O P Q R S T U V W X Y
```

A Vigenère tableau

ATTACK AT DAWN, will be enciphered by a process that starts by writing the keyword over the plaintext message as follows:

CRY P TOLOGYCRYPTOLOGY
ATTACKATDAWN

The ciphertext is now created from the tableau by selecting the letter from the tableau that is at the intersection of the row given by the keyword letter and the column given by the plaintext letter. In the example this process produces the ciphertext.

C K R P V Y L H J Y Y E

Note that this ciphertext, either with or without the original word spacings, has a different character than that of the Caesar cipher in that it tends to mask the frequency of letter usage in the language. For example, the ciphertext employs three uses of Y, but each one represents different letters in the plaintext. Also, there are three uses of T in the plaintext, but they are represented by three different letters in the ciphertext.

Decipherment is accomplished simply by repeatedly writing the keyword above the ciphertext as follows:

C R Y P T O L O G Y C R Y P T O L O G Y

C K R P V Y L H J Y Y E

Next, the correspondent would move across each row identified by a keyword letter until the associated ciphertext letter is located. The corresponding plaintext letter will head the column containing the ciphertext letter.

The cryptographer would soon start to make even more changes in the encipherment process to complicate the cryptanalyst's job. For example, he or she would hide the number of letters in a given plaintext word by making all of the groups of ciphertext the same length, using multiple alphabets, changing the key during the course of the message, etc. As one of his or her first changes, the cryptographer might even use numerals instead of letters, or place the message in a code prior to the encipherment.[4]

In fact, in the early use of the Baudot code, the cryptographic key was applied directly to the plaintext. But it was not until the introduction of the start-stop mode of teletype that mechanical encipherment became both easy and popular. A technique similar to the Baudot code is still used in computers today with a popular code known as the American Standard Code for Information Interchange (ASCII). This particular code uses 8-bit binary numbers to represent the alphabet, numerals, punctuation, functions, etc. There are 256 unique representations possible.

All ciphers do not by any means have the same basic character. The previous discussion focused on substitution ciphers, where one letter was replaced by another. Another common technique is the transposition cipher where the same letters (or their representations) are used, but their placement in the communication is changed. Perhaps the simplest example of this type of cipher would be just writing the message backwards. Many other techniques, some quite elaborate, can be used. Obviously, this type of cipher poses a completely different type of problem to the cryptanalyst. Other methods use combinations of both substitution and transposition. The potential types of complications seem to be endless.

## Is There Something Particularly Special About Voice?

Our ability to speak and understand each other is absolutely amazing. Humans produce individualized speech patterns in many languages. We not only understand each other, but also recognize speakers and provide complex interpretations of emotions and nuances in speech pattern that are difficult to analyze and quantify. We have all experienced the complexity of human speech. It is extremely difficult to measure and quantify all of the features of the spoken word.

Speech research remains important today. From the time of Alexander Graham Bell until the present, communications researchers have been exploring ways to analyze and transmit speech. This process has encouraged the investigation of many related topics, such as the ability to accurately measure the intelligibility of the spoken word.

In this simplified example, the electronic signal representing voice is created by the speech air-pressure wave, which generates an analog waveform by means

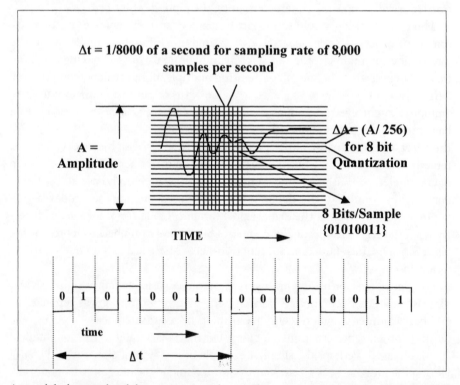

A simplified example of the conversion of an analog voice signal to a digital representation. In this example, the data rate will be 64,000 bps because the amplitude of the voice signal is represented by 8 bits of data every ⅛₀₀₀th of a second.

of a microphone. Let's say that the communications system engineer wants to transform the voice signal into a digital format to take advantage of encipherment by digital means (similar in some ways to what we have discussed for digital printer signals). For this waveform to be transformed directly into a digital signal, it would be encoded by sampling the amplitude of the analog signal at periodic time increments. For this example, 8 bits are selected for each amplitude measurement. Because 8 bits will produce 256 digital representations, each sample is quantified to an accuracy of $\frac{1}{256}$ of the maximum. The sampling rate required to avoid distortion must be at least twice the highest frequency component of the analog signal.[5] Therefore, if we wish to reconstruct the voice signal to a limit of, say, 4,000 cycles/second (hertz), a sampling rate of not less than 8,000 samples per second must be used. Just for reference, compact music disks (CDs) allocate 16 bits per sample. However, for our example, using 8 bits per sample at 8,000 samples per second results in a minimum sample rate of 64,000 bits per second. This would require far too much transmission bandwidth in many communication systems.

Methods to reduce the required electronic communications bandwidth to something more like that used for the transmission of the original analog signal have been under investigation for a long time. One successful example was mentioned in chapter 7 (the CELP method and the resulting Federal Standard 1016). There are others. Once encoded, digital encipherment algorithms may be employed. Some of these may again change the requirements for communication bandwidth. Many good choices are available. The fundamental goal is to preserve the ability of the communicators to not only understand the spoken word but also retain the ability to interpret the nuances of the voice regardless of the technology used in the transmission and encipherment/decipherment processes. Now consider the problem such systems present to the cryptanalyst.

We have implied that knowledge of the language is one of the most useful aids to cryptanalysts who work on written materials. Although spoken languages may also contain many measurable differences, these differences are obviously of a different character than those that appear in the written word. No obvious aids are to be derived from sentence structures, spelling rules, or similar information features. Voice signals do indeed present special problems in both the enciphering and deciphering processes.

## Modern Digital Cryptographic Systems

The modern world is going digital. Information is stored and retrieved from computers represented by an organized series of 1s and 0s. Transfer of information over modern communications media such as fiber-optic cable is accomplished by

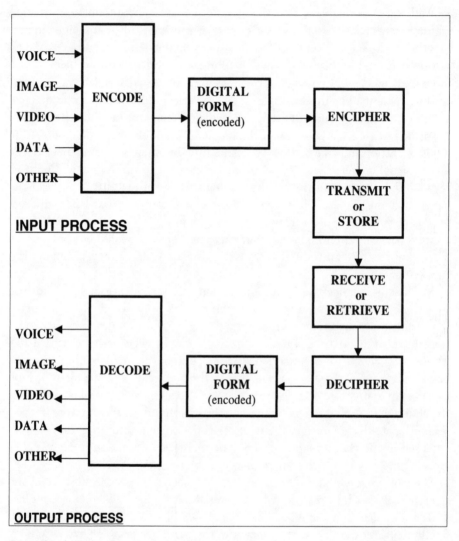

Generalized process flow

standardized formatting of digital representations. In general, information is stored and transported by digital representations that are derived from voice, graphics, etc. The above example of voice encoding from the analog to digital form demonstrates a conversion process. With the modern world storing and transporting digital representations, ciphers scrambling ones and zeroes can accommodate a variety of information sources.

Without exception, this general process can encode any information source as a binary sequence of 1s and 0s. The exact way in which this is accomplished is a function of the form of the information source and the desire to minimize any distortion in the encoding-decoding activity. Voice, graphics, etc., are encoded by a series of standards that take in consideration the unique requirements of the information source. Once the source has been placed in a digital form, the system can encipher or scramble the bits, which protects the information during storage or transport. The received enciphered bits are deciphered recovering the original digital form. Decoding the digital form recovers the information in its original form.

## Is There More Than One Basic Type of Encipherment System?

There are two fundamentally different types of encipherment systems employed today. They can be combined in various ways, but for this introduction we will examine only two.

The first type—the symmetrical, secret-key system—has the longest history. This basic type of system requires a controlled and secure method of both producing and distributing the secret keys. For a large system, this is an expensive process. The keys require periodic updating, and the probability of compromise increases as the number of users increases. Nevertheless, this remains the classical system.

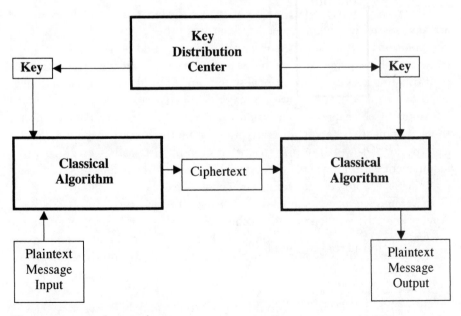

Classic symmetrical, secret-key system

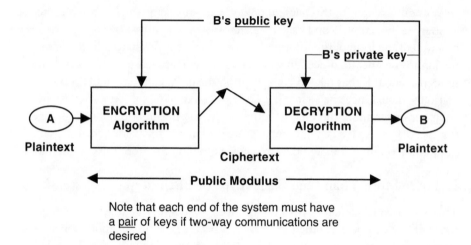

Note that each end of the system must have a <u>pair</u> of keys if two-way communications are desired

Model of a public-key system


A second type of system is public-key cryptography, or asymmetric cryptography. It is fundamentally different from the symmetrical, secret-key system in its mode of operation and the underlying mathematics.

The public-key cryptosystems do not change the fact that the basic security of any cryptographic scheme depends primarily on the length of the key and the computational difficulty of breaking the cipher. Based on the security of the ciphertext alone, public-key systems have no inherent advantage. The difficulties of distributing keys in a conventional system, and most likely the issues surrounding the control of such keys, were a major factor that prompted work on public-key systems (see chapter 4 for a brief discussion of this concept). Fundamentally, these systems use one key for encryption and a different, yet related, key for decryption. It is worth noting that what cryptologists call "secrecy" is still a requirement within the public-key system. In concept, the required secrecy is easier to manage, enforce, and monitor in a public-key system.

In a simplified model of a public key system, if A wishes to send B a message, A must know B's public key and another public piece of information, called the network's modulus. The encryption algorithm uses this combination and creates the ciphertext, which is delivered to the decryption algorithm where B's private key is used to again produce plain text. The reverse process is required to produce two-way communication.

The major distinction between this type of system and the conventional (symmetrical, secret-key) system is that nothing either secret or private must be shared between the two correspondents before they begin the communications process.

Unlike the symmetrical secret-key system, when using the public-key system, the sender must separately encrypt the message for each recipient, because of the special mathematical relationship among all of the users' public and private keys. This feature requires significant computer and communications capability. It does not cause an operational problem in many applications; it is the general type of system that most current Internet applications use. In one sense, a public-key cryptography system is economical because, although it requires secret keys, they do not need to be transmitted between users. On the other hand, the computations that users must use to encipher and decipher a message are rather extensive and limit the systems to relatively short messages. As with any cryptologic system, public-key cryptography requires users to make technical choices and it has security hazards, but it also has distinct advantages.

Deciding whether the advantages of one particular system make it useable in the face of the known disadvantages and threats is usually the job of a team of cryptographers, cryptanalysts, and doctrinal evaluators (cryptanalysts of sorts) who engage in risk-analysis studies. Risk analysis is another component of the cryptologic arts and sciences.

Are there uses for cryptographic systems other than the classic one of enciphering messages? More widely available technology in our three fields of communications, computers, and cryptology has prompted many additional applications of cryptologic techniques. A simplified view of five examples of these applications will give an idea of their nature, although many variants exist, and others are in constant development.

An early noncommunications application of cryptologic techniques was in identification, friend or foe (IFF) systems for military services. In one example, as a search radar would illuminate a potential target and send an enciphered message to interrogate the target that message would be deciphered by the target system that would, in turn, reply automatically with another enciphered message verifying its identity. These systems are now technically complex, but even the early applications served a very important function in separating friends from foe in, for example, air-to-air and ground-to-air engagements. Systems similar to the military versions are now in use in most nations' air traffic control systems.

The command and control systems for satellites and space probes have provided many uses for cryptologic systems. The authenticity of a command must be automatically verified to prevent either accidental or intentional interference with the command systems of these expensive (and important) resources. Cryptography can be used to verify the commands and protect against intentional interference (jamming).

The public-key system offers another important feature. If an electronic message is enciphered using the private key, it can only be deciphered by the associated public key. This feature plays an important role in establishing an electronic signature for plaintext document exchange. When a document is received and the authenticity of the sender needs to be established, an attached file—containing selected information that the recipient can verify is enciphered using the sender's private key—is deciphered using the public key, thereby verifying the sender, who is the only one who should know the private key. Sometimes, the communicators need to take additional steps to ensure that an electronic signature is satisfactory. In particular, nonrepudiation by the sender (meaning that the sender cannot deny the origin of the information) is ensured if it can be proved that the document was not altered in transit. Electronic signature systems in use today have solved these problems and have increased the efficiency of most transactions of value (for example, banking).

More traditional symmetrical encryption systems have incorporated public-key systems to help distribute the required secret keys. This capability, particularly useful in large networks, takes advantage of many public-key systems' ability to be initiated without the exchange of secret information, but they also have some operational disadvantages. The computational capability requirements and the fact that each recipient needs an individual message encryption means that public-key systems tend to be significantly slower for long messages than a symmetrical secret-key system. When the two system types are combined, the finest features of each can be used to best advantage. For example, a typical hybrid application could involve using the public-key system to send an encrypted secret key to a correspondent (or set of correspondents). Then, at each terminal the user would decrypt the secret key (using his or her public key) and subsequently install it electronically in equipment suited for a symmetrical secret-key system operation. Once the communications network has been supplied with this secret key, it could be used in the classic way, allowing network members to communicate with each other efficiently. In such applications, risk analysts would probably require that the use of the secret key be confined to only one communications session.

Many possible variations of this generalized situation are possible. Although it may require complex equipment, this type of hybrid system for key distribution can be very useful. Where appropriate, such as in advanced voice-security systems, this technique can permit an economical and flexible system to distribute secret keying materials to large networks in a short period of time. The techniques used to generate the secret key remain important, and the integrity of the network must be maintained. Again, cryptographic techniques, such as digital signatures, can be used to aid in these processes.

With the spread of the use of computer systems and their incorporation into networks some challenging security concerns emerged. A detailed discussion of these concerns is beyond the scope of this book. It should obvious, however, that the process of providing ensured service from a complex network of subsystems, while ensuring easy interoperability, has demanded international cooperation in the development of technical standards. Some of the references for this chapter offer good introductions to the problems of providing what has come to be known as information assurance. In 1978, the International Organization for Standardization (ISO) proposed a reference model for structuring large networked systems. Many designers and operators have accepted this reference model (ISO-RM) for use. The systems are "layered" in the sense that basic functions are described regardless of whether they are accomplished in hardware or software. Security tools (or mechanisms) are also described within the standards. Many of these tools incorporate cryptologic functions. The names of the eight mechanisms used in these standards are generally self-explanatory. The mechanisms (or tools) are encipherment, digital signature, access control, data integrity, authentication exchange, traffic padding (used to disguise the presence or absence of an exchange), routing control, and notarization (assurance provision from a trusted third party). The names alone tell the story of the spread of cryptology into communications and computer systems.

Not all modern uses are confined to large information processing systems. Cryptologic techniques are used in some modern digital cellular phone systems and in remote access devices for automobiles, garage door openers, and similar household devices.

The evolution of communications and computers has supported the growth in sophisticated ciphers and related techniques. These uses are spreading.

## Good Sources of Additional Information

The references cited in previous chapters offer sources of further information. These sources and some additional books are contained in the bibliography. A number of Internet newsgroups specialize in cryptography and information security matters.

A particularly interesting organization called the American Cryptogram Association (ACA), a testimony to the wide appeal of the topic, is a source of educational material. ACA was established in 1929 by hobbyists as an outgrowth of their interest in puzzles and other features on cryptology in fiction magazines, and the association published a textbook on cryptanalysis in 1939. It has since published many other booklets and papers on cryptography-related subjects. Its members also provide recommendations on reference materials of many sorts.

With a worldwide membership of nearly a thousand, ACA publishes a bimonthly journal featuring articles on many topics. Most of the journal's offerings can be enjoyed with paper and pencil although it does have a segment on the use of software for personal computers. One segment focuses on introducing cryptography to children and beginners. Further information can be obtained from the ACA Web site.

*Cryptologia* is an unclassified scholarly journal devoted to cryptology. First published in 1977, it covers topics including history, codes and ciphers, mathematics, computer security, and cipher devices. It also features book reviews on the subject. The journal, although not a U.S. government publication, is produced and published at the United States Military Academy.

In 2003, the IEEE Computer Society initiated a new journal, *IEEE Security & Privacy*. This is a new effort to serve the professionals who are engaged in all phases of cryptologic activities in both the computer security and privacy fields. It will provide an opportunity for peer-reviewed publications in this expanding area of technical interest.

Contrary to just twenty years ago, much cryptology-related information, particularly concerning its technology, is now publicly available.

# Appendix B
## THE ORIGINS OF NSA[1]

Although "code making and breaking" are ancient practices, modern cryptologic communications intelligence activities in the United States date from the World War I period and radio communications technology. In 1917 and 1918, the U.S. Army created, within the Military Intelligence Division (MID), the Cipher Bureau (MI-8) under Herbert O. Yardley. MID assisted the radio intelligence units in the American Expeditionary Forces and in 1918 created the Radio Intelligence Service for operations along the Mexican border. The Navy had established a modest effort, but it was absorbed, by mutual agreement in 1918, into Yardley's post-war civilian "Black Chamber."

The Army (and State Department) continued to support Yardley until the termination of his Black Chamber in 1929. Army continuity was assumed, however, in the small Signal Intelligence Service under the direction of William F. Friedman. The Navy's cryptanalytic function reappeared formally in 1924 in the "research desk" under Laurance F. Safford in the Code and Signal Section, OP-20-G, within the Office of Naval Communications. While emphasis was on the security of U.S. military communications (COMSEC), both organizations developed radio intercept, radio direction finding, and processing capabilities prior to World War II; they achieved particular successes against Japanese diplomatic communications. Exploitation successes of their respective counterpart services had to await the shift of resources until after hostilities commenced. However, wartime successes by the United States and Britain proved the value of

COMINT to military and political leaders, and, as a result, both service organizations expanded greatly in terms of manpower resources and equipment.

In the later stages of the war, the services created a coordinating body to facilitate COMINT cooperation, the Army-Navy Communications Intelligence Board (ANCIB) with a subordinate coordinating committee (ANCICC). These became instruments for negotiating joint post-war arrangements. In late 1945, with the addition of the Department of State to its membership, the ANCIB became the State-Army-Navy Communications Intelligence Board (STANCIB). STANCIB evolved in 1946 into the United States Communications Intelligence Board (USCIB), which added the FBI as a member.

With the passage of the National Security Act of 1947, Congress reinforced the direction in which the intelligence community was moving—toward increased centralization—and built the framework for a modern national security structure. Among other things, the act established the National Security Council (NCS) and the Central Intelligence Agency (CIA). The CIA became a member of USCIB, which received a new charter as the highest national COMINT authority in the form of an NCSC Intelligence Directive, NSCID No. 9, dated July 1948.

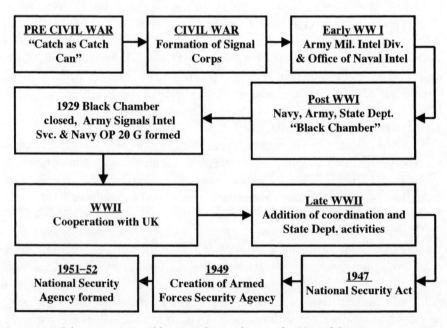

Overview of the organizational history of cryptology in the United States

As the Air Force sought to expand its cryptologic organization, Secretary of Defense James V. Forrestal contemplated cutting defense expenditures. One solution was a unified cryptologic agency. He appointed a special board under Rear Adm. Earl E. Stone, Director of Naval Communications, to formulate a plan for merging all military COMINT and COMSEC activities and resources into a single agency. Only the Army favored the Stone board's recommendations for merger at this time, and the plan was shelved.

In 1949, a new Secretary of Defense, Louis A. Johnson, also seeking ways to economize, reviewed the Stone board's report and began to take steps for its implementation. After much discussion among the services regarding the concept of merger, on May, 20, 1949, Secretary Johnson ordered the issuance of JCS Directive 2010. This directive established the Armed Forces Security Agency (AFSA), which had as its mission the conduct of communications intelligence and communications security activities within the National Military Establishment. AFSA thus had the actual responsibility for running COMINT and COMSEC operations, excluding only those that were delegated individually to the Army, Navy, and Air Force. The JCS directive also established an advisory council within the AFSA structure. Known for a time as the Armed Forces Communications Intelligence Advisory Council (AFCIAC), it later was renamed Armed Forces Security Agency Council (AFSAC). The organization became the mechanism through which AFSA reported to the JCS.

On July 15, 1949, Admiral Stone became AFSA's first director, appointed by the JCS. By January 1950, the Army and Navy cryptologic organizations had transferred enough civilian and military personnel, as well as equipment, so that AFSA could operate. AFSA did not, however, have its own facilities.

Admiral Stone was succeeded in 1951 by Maj. Gen. Ralph J. Canine, U.S. Army. By this time, various difficulties in defining powers and areas of jurisdiction were painfully obvious. Further, both directors experienced grave difficulties in obtaining the Advisory Council's approval of proposed courses of action because of AFSAC's policy requiring unanimous decisions. Finally, the potentialities of expanding technical COMINT capabilities of the late 1940s could not always be realized. During the Korean War the quality of strategic intelligence derived from COMINT fell below that which had been provided in World War II. Consumers were disappointed and increasingly critical. By late 1951, AFSA had clashed with the service cryptologic agencies, with consumers, with CIA, and with the State Department, although not all at one time or on one issue. Despite the intentions, AFSA had in fact become a fourth military cryptologic agency.

On December 13, 1951, President Truman ordered a searching analysis to be conducted by a special committee to be named by the Secretaries of State and Defense, aided by the Director of Central Intelligence. Chaired by George

Brownell, an eminent New York lawyer, the Brownell Committee surveyed the situation and in June recommended that a unified COMINT agency receive greater powers commensurate with clearly defined responsibilities. It also advised that the agency be freed of the crippling line of subordination through AFSAC to the JCS and, instead, be directly subordinate to the Secretary of Defense, acting with the Secretary of State on behalf of the NSC. It further proposed that the unified agency be controlled in policy matters by a reconstituted USCIB, under the chairmanship of the Director of Central Intelligence, in which the representation of military and nonmilitary intelligence interests would be evenly balanced.

In October 1952, the President and National Security Council adopted most of the Brownell Committee's recommendations and issued a revised version of NSCID No. 9 on October 24, 1952.

A mingling of military and nonmilitary interests was expressed in the word "national." The production of COMINT was declared to be a national responsibility. In place of an Armed Forces Security Agency, the U.S. government was to have a National Security Agency, an organization with the same resources plus a new charter. The AFSA Council, while not specifically abolished, thus had the agency pulled out from under it. The Joint Chiefs of Staff were no longer in the chain-of-command. The Director, NSA, reported to the Secretary of Defense through a unit in the latter's office that dealt with sensitive operations. The Secretary himself was declared to be the executive agent of the government for COMINT and subordinate to a special committee for the NSC, of which he and the Secretary of State were the two members and the Director of Central Intelligence was an advisor.

The Secretary of Defense was instructed to delegate his COMINT responsibilities to the Director of NSA, and to entrust to him operational and technical control of all U.S. military COMINT collection and production resources. The Director, NSA, was ordered to bring about the most effective, unified application of all U.S. resources for producing COMINT to meet requirements approved by USCIB. In addition, the DIRNSA was ordered to assume the COMSEC responsibilities previously assigned to AFSA.

Promulgation of NSCID No. 9 brought about a greater participation by civilian members (CIA and State) of the community in the COMINT process. At the same time it was recognition of the necessity for more centralized technical operations.

On November 4, 1952, General Canine became the first Director, NSA. In 1957, NSA consolidated its headquarters operations at Fort George G. Meade, Maryland.

A current description of the responsibilities of the NSA is contained in Executive Order 12333 of December 4, 1981. This document describes the two national missions of the NSA and the Central Security Service (CSS) as follows:[2]

The foreign signals intelligence or SIGINT mission allows for an effective, unified organization and control of all foreign signals collection and processing activities of the United States. NSA is authorized to produce SIGINT in accordance with objectives, requirements, and priorities established by the Director of Central Intelligence with the advice of the National Foreign Intelligence Board.

The information systems security or INFOSEC mission provides leadership, products, technical advice, and services to protect classified and unclassified national security systems against exploitation through interception, unauthorized access, or related technical intelligence threats. This mission also supports the Director, NSA in fulfilling his responsibilities as Executive Agency for interagency operations security (OPSEC) training.

# NOTES

## Foreword

1. Dr. Perry has been the secretary of defense (1994–97), the deputy secretary of defense (1993–94), and the undersecretary of defense for Research and Engineering (1977–81). He was a member of the NSA Scientific Advisory Board for many years. He is currently a senior fellow at the Hoover Institution, is a professor in the School of Engineering at Stanford University, and holds a wide variety of positions in industry.

## Preface

1. The National Cryptologic Museum is a museum of the U.S. Department of Defense. Opened to the public in 1996 and located near the headquarters of the National Security Agency in Fort Meade, Maryland, it offers a wide variety of educational exhibits about cryptology. We have all been involved with this museum and recommend it highly.

## Chapter 1. Overview

1. Nathan Rosenberg, Ralph Landau, and David C. Mowery, *Technology and the Wealth of Nations*, 1.
2. For a good discussion of the issues, see *Balancing the National Interest* (Washington, D.C.: National Academy Press, 1987).
3. Several sources have been used for this condensed story. They include David Kahn, *The Codebreakers* (New York: Scribner, 1996); David Stafford, *Churchill and Secret Service* (Woodstock, NY: Overlook, 1998); Michael Smith, *Station X* (New York: TV Books, 1999); and Stephen Budianski, *Battle of Wits* (New York: Free Press, 2000).
4. This summary has been derived from J. V. Boone and R. R. Peterson, *The Start of the Digital Revolution: SIGSALY, Secure Digital Voice Communications in World War II* (Fort Meade, MD: Center for Cryptologic History, National Security Agency, 2000).

## Chapter 2. 1200–1800: The Introduction of Mechanical Aids

1. Robert Silverberg, *The Longest Voyage* (New York: The Bobbs-Merrill Co., 1972).
2. James R. Newman, ed., *The World of Mathematics*, vol. 1 (New York: Simon and Schuster, 1956), 442.
3. Will Durant, *The Story of Civilization: Part IV The Age of Faith* (New York: Simon and Schuster, 1950), 906.

4. Kahn, *The Codebreakers*, 71–672. This book contains detailed descriptions of many types of cryptographic systems and is the primary source of much of this summary material.

5. Background on this example, and many other interesting examples of cryptology in early American history, is found in Ralph E. Weber, *Masked Dispatches: Cryptograms and Cryptology in American History, 1775–1900* (Fort Meade, MD: Center for Cryptologic History, National Security Agency, 1993).

6. Ibid., 59.

7. Ibid., 61.

8. Ibid., 83–86.

An additional source of related information is also available in Ralph E. Weber, *United States Diplomatic Codes and Ciphers, 1775–1938* (Chicago: Precedent Publishing, Inc., 1979).

## Chapter 3. 1800–1895: The Introduction of the Telegraph, the Telephone, and Mechanical Computing Aids

1. For an interesting and extensive description of this story see Mark Urban, *The Man Who Broke Napoleon's Codes* (New York: Harper Collins, 2001).

2. Doron Swade, *The Difference Engine* (New York: Penguin Books, 2000). This very readable book tells the story of Babbage's successes and failures. The author, a primary force behind the efforts to complete the construction of Babbage's more advanced designs, relates many insights into that process as well as the colorful life of Charles Babbage.

3. This is not an original observation; however, it is unclear who should be credited for first noting how important this trend would be. Professor and technology critic Neil Postman (1931–2003) discussed the topic in his book, *Technopoly: The Surrender of Culture to Technology* (New York: Alfred A. Knopf, 1992). He notes on page 67 that "The telegraph removed space as an inevitable constraint on the movement of information, and, for the fist time transportation and communications were disengaged from each other." The telegraph permitted many new human activities and promised new technical capabilities.

4. The frequency of letters differs by language group. In addition, even in English, the measure changes depending on the extent of the vocabulary in use. Nevertheless, Morse's observations produced an effective code.

5. Kahn, *The Codebreakers*, 217.

6. For a basic understanding of the extent to which many communications techniques were used in the Civil War, see Francis Trevelyan Miller, ed., *The Photographic History of the Civil War*, vol. 8 (New York: The Review of Reviews Co., 1912). This is also the direct source of the quotes from Generals Grant and Sherman.

   Insights into the use of the telegraph as well as a personal account of the progress of the war are clearly stated in a recent book edited by Donald E. Markle,

*The Telegraph Goes to War: The Personal Diary of David Homer Bates, Lincoln's Telegraph Operator* (Hamilton, NY: Edmonston, 2003). This book describes the dynamics of the evolving command-and-control uses of the telegraph.

7. For a thoughtful examination of this topic and other aspects of the contribution of the Civil War to modern warfare, see Edward Hagerman, *The American Civil War and the Origins of Modern Warfare* (Bloomington: Indiana University Press, 1988).

An interesting and authoritative treatment of military intelligence in the Civil War, including that derived from communications, is Edwin C. Fishel, *The Secret War for the Union: The Untold Story of Military Intelligence in the Civil War* (Boston: Houghton Mifflin Co., 1996).

8. Examples of all of these activities, particularly those of the Canadian George Ellsworth, who was a telegrapher for the Confederate forces of Col. John H. Morgan, are contained in William R. Plum, *The Military Telegraph during the Civil War in the United States* (Chicago: Jansen, McClurg and Co., 1882), 193–202.

9. Firsthand accounts of Lincoln's activities in this area are contained in David Homer Bates, *Lincoln in the Telegraph Office* (New York: Century, 1907).

10. A description of the business, political, and technical efforts associated with this adventure can be found in John Steel Gordon, *A Thread Across the Ocean: The Heroic Story of the Transatlantic Cable* (New York: Walker & Co., 2002).

# Chapter 4. 1895–1939: The Introduction of Radio Stimulates New Applications

1. "1897 Transactions of the American Institute of Electrical Engineers," *Wireless Telegraphy*, December 1897

2. The amazing story of the Zimmerman telegram is too important to summarize here. We recommend the story as told in Kahn, *The Codebreakers*, 286–97.

3. Ibid., 297.

4. Ibid., 415–20.

5. For an accurate and brief description of the basic ENIGMA encryption process, see A. Ray Miller, *The Cryptographic Mathematics of Enigma* (Fort Meade, MD: Center for Cryptologic History, National Security Agency, 1999). Additional insights may be obtained from chapter 4 of Simon Singh, *The Code Book* (New York: Doubleday, 1999).

6. Biographical material on Rowlett, Friedman, and a few other early American cryptographers is contained in *Pioneers in U.S. Cryptology*, a brochure available from the Center for Cryptologic History, National Security Agency.

7. For more detailed information on the wired-rotor machines, see Steve Kelly, *Big Machines* (Laguna Hills, CA: Aegean Park Press, 2001).

8. The full title of this paper is *On Computable Numbers with an Application to the Entscheidungsproblem*. It was written in 1936 and, after much review, was published in 1937 by the London Mathematical Society.

## Chapter 5. Mid-1930s–1950: World War II Accelerates Developments in All Fields

1. For a firsthand overview of this analytic feat and the associated personal interactions, see Frank B. Rowlett, *The Story of Magic*.
2. For an overview of the operation of the BOMBE, see Budianski, *Battle of Wits*, 125–31. For an excellent overview of the history and operation of the BOMBE, see Jennifer Wilcox, *Solving the Enigma: History of the Cryptanalytic BOMBE* (Ft. Meade, MD: Center for Cryptologic History, National Security Agency, 2002).
3. Jim DeBrosse, "Dayton's Code Breakers," *Dayton Daily News* series, February–August 2001.
4. Quote from U.S. Naval Cryptologic Veterans Association (Paducah, KY: Turner Publishing Co., 1996), 43.
5. For more detail of this complex story, see Carl Boyd, *Hitler's Japanese Confidant: General Oshima Hiroshi and MAGIC* (Lawrence: University of Kansas, 1993).
6. For more detail, see Boone and Peterson, *The Start of the Digital Revolution*.
7. A more complete version of this complex story is found in Kahn, *The Codebreakers*, 425–32.
8. For a more detailed description of COLOSSUS and the events leading up to its invention, see Raul Rojas and Ulf Hashagen, eds., *The First Computers, History and Architectures* (Cambridge, MA: MIT Press, 2000), 351–64. This segment of the book was written by Anthony Sale, who was the original director of the Bletchley Park trust that established a museum in Bletchley Park to commemorate the World War II cryptologic work performed there.
9. For more detail, see David J. Crawford and Philip E. Fox, "The Autoscritcher and Superscritcher: Aids to Cryptanalysis of the German Enigma Cipher Machine, 1944–1946," *IEEE Annals of the History of Computing*, vol. 14, no. 3 (1992): 9,322.
   For some other examples of special equipments of this generation, see appendix E in Budiansky, *Battle of Wits*.
10. For an interesting and complete description of this milestone program, see Scott McCartney, *ENIAC*.
11. For further information on the remarkable career and contributions of computer scientist and mathematician Grace Hopper, see Williams, Kathleen Broome, *Grace Hopper: Admiral of the Cyber Sea* (Annapolis, MD: Naval Institute Press, 2004).
12. The important role of the U.S. Navy's cryptologic activities in the early formation of the computer industry in America is illustrated in an article by Colin Burke titled "An Introduction to a Historic Computer Document: The 1946 Pendergrass Report—Cryptanalysis and the Digital Computer" in *Cryptologia*, vol. XVIII, no. 2 (April 1993). This article also implies the important connection between the Navy experiences at Bletchley Park and their desire to promote work on high-speed computing machines for cryptologic purposes both during and after the war.
13. This paper has been published in many forms, but the first formal publication was in *The Bell System Technical Journal*, vol. 27 (July and October, 1948): 379–423, 623–56.

## Chapter 6. 1950–1969: The Introduction of Solid-State Electronics and Satellite Technologies

1. A good example of the attention given to the administration of cryptographic materials and processes is the following general order of the Civil War era.

War Department

Washington City, January 1st, 1864

ORDERED:

That the cipher books issued by the Superintendent of Military Telegraphs be entrusted only to the care of telegraph experts, selected for the duty by the Superintendent of Telegraphs, and approved and appointed by the Secretary of War for duty at the respective headquarters of the Military Departments, and to accompany the armies in the field. The ciphers furnished for this purpose are not to be imparted to any one, but will be kept by one operator to whom they are entrusted, in strict confidence, and he will be held responsible for their proper use. They will neither be copied nor used by any other person, without special permission from the Secretary of War. Generals commanding will report to the War Department any default of duty by the cipher operator, but will not allow any staff or other officer to interfere with the operators in the discharge of their duties.

By Order of the Secretary of War.

Official: T. S. Bowers, A.A.G.

(Source: Plum, *The Military Telegraph during the Civil War in the United States*)

2. For a good description of the organizational disputes and, to some extent, the role that differing telegraphic technologies played in them, see Hagerman, *The American Civil War and the Origins of Modern Warfare*.
3. Information for this segment has been obtained from a much more complete document, M. H. Klein, *Security for Record Communications: The TCS KW-26* (Fort Meade, MD: Center for Cryptologic History, National Security Agency, 2002).
4. Arthur Schawlow and Charles Townes, "Infrared and Optical Masers," *Physical Review* vol. 112 (December 1958):1,940–49.

## Chapter 7. 1970–2003: Extended Networking Concepts Bring Closer Integration to All Three Technologies

1. For examples of the complexities of espionage, see Pete Earley, *Family of Spies: Inside the John Walker Spy Ring* (repr., New York: Bantam Books, 1993).
2. A nonreversible mathematical function is one that can easily be executed in one direction, but is very difficult, if not impossible, to reverse by later analysis without knowing the factors specifically involved in the first process. For example, it is easy

to multiply two large prime numbers and obtain the product, but it is very difficult to examine that product and determine what the two original prime numbers were.

3. A brief technical definition of CTAK is given in Carl H. Meyer and Steven M. Matyas, *Cryptography* (New York: Wiley-Interscience, 1982), 88–91.

4. For additional data, see the U.S. Department of Justice Web site, www.usdoj.gov, for a segment on "Privacy Act Overview."

5. A description of the DES algorithm is widely available. One of the best sources is the National Institute of Standards and Technology publication Federal Information Processing Standards Publication 46-2 (FPIS PUB 46–2), December 30, 1993. An excellent description of how the system works is found in Dorothy Denning, *Cryptography and Data Security* (Reading, MA: Addison-Wesley Publishing Co., 1983).

6. Micha Schwartz, *Telecommunications Networks, Protocols, Modeling and Analysis* (New York: Pearson Education, 1986), 6. This excellent book presents a detailed overview of many of the engineering considerations that surround the design of modern communications networks. The first book to treat both voice and data networks, it remains a good reference on the subject.

7. For a good nontechnical description of the achievements and conflicts on this subject, see Steven Levy, *Crypto* (New York: Viking Penguin, 2001).

8. Now that this fact is understood, many good references explain the process. Two are Gustavus Simmons, *Contemporary Cryptology* (Piscataway, NJ: IEEE Press, 1992) and Meyer and Matyas, *Cryptography*.

9. CELP is a complex signal-processing scheme. For those who are interested, it is described in the Federal Standard itself, but an early explanatory article is Joseph P. Campbell Jr., Thomas E. Tremain, and Vanoy C. Welch, "The Federal Standard 1016 4800 bps CELP Voice Coder," *Digital Signal Processing* 1, no. 3 (1991): 145–55.

10. Carver Mead and Lynn Conway, *Introduction to VLSI Systems*, v.

11. A good introduction to this topic can be obtained from George Johnson *A Shortcut through Time: The Path to a Quantum* (New York: Alfred A. Knopf/Random House, 2003). This unique book is written specifically for the nonspecialist who is interested in gaining an understanding of how a potentially revolutionary technology may work, as well as the possible impact of using that capability.

12. Please see the id Quantique Web site, www.idquantique.com/company.

## Chapter 8. Summary

1. An excellent description of this type of activity is contained in William R. Plum, *The Military Telegraph during the Civil War in the United States*. This firsthand account of the subject is hard to find but provides detailed examples.

2. C. E. Shannon, "Communication Theory of Secrecy Systems," *Bell Systems Technical Journal* 28 (October 1949): 656–715; C. E. Shannon. "A Mathematical Theory of Communications." *Bell Systems Technical Journal* 27 (July and October 1948): 379–423, 623–56.

3. Hendry, John, *Innovating for Failure: Government Policy and the Early British Computer Industry* (Cambridge, MA: The MIT Press, 1990). This work examines the factors that influenced the evolution of the computer industries in both the United States and Britain. It is a part of the MIT series on the history of computing, edited by I. Bernard Cohen and William Aspray, which is a major contribution to the history of this field.

4. Arthur C. Clarke eventually became a prolific science fiction writer. He invented the idea of geosynchronous communications systems in his article "Extra-Terrestrial Relays: Can Rocket Stations Give World-wide Radio Coverage?" *Wireless World* (October 1945): 305–8. Although he later graduated from Kings College, London, with honors in physics and mathematics, in 1948 he wrote a clear, technically accurate description of the advantages of using satellite-borne systems for communications purposes while on active duty from 1941 to 1946. Generally recognized as the inventor of this idea, he has been given many international honors for his foresight.

5. Richard N. Haass, "Supporting US Foreign Policy in the Post-9/11 World," *Studies in Intelligence* 46, no. 3 (2002), 1–13.

6. See an excellent treatment of this subject in James Utterback, *Mastering the Dynamics of Innovation* (Boston: Harvard Business School Press, 1994).

7. From Atsushi Akera and Frederik Nebeker, *From 0 to 1: An Authoritative History of Modern Computing* (New York: Oxford University Press, 2002), 200.

8. Hendry, *Innovating for Failure: Government Policy and the Early British Computer Industry*.

9. Juris Hartmanis and Herbert Lin, eds, *Computing the Future: A Broader Agenda for Computer Science and Engineering* (Washington, DC: National Academy Press, 1992).

10. Thomas L. Friedman, *The Lexus and the Olive Tree: Understanding Globalization* (New York: Anchor Books, 2000), 8.

# Appendix A: Introduction to Cryptology

1. See Kahn, *The Codebreakers*, chapter 2, for a great tour through the early years of cryptography.

2. Dr. Abrahm Sinkov (1907–1998) was born in Philadelphia of Russian immigrants. He grew up in Brooklyn and earned a B.S. in mathematics from the City College of New York. He was teaching in the New York school system when he was recruited by William Friedman into the Army Signal Intelligence Service in 1930. He received a Ph.D. in mathematics from George Washington University in 1933. He became a premier cryptologic practitioner in the United States, serving in many positions. Not only his mathematical talent, but also his organizational and leadership skills were essential in developing intelligence relationships with Australia that were extremely important during World War II, particularly the war in the Pacific.

After the war, Dr. Sinkov continued to work at AFSA and NSA until he retired from government service in 1962. He was appointed professor of mathematics at Arizona State University where he worked until his second retirement. While at Arizona State, he wrote *Elementary Cryptanalysis, A Mathematical Approach* (Washington, DC: Mathematical Association of America, 1966), which was published in 1966. This was one of the first books published on the subject in the United States. It was still in print at the time of his death in 1998.

3. Abraham Sinkov, *Elementary Cryptanalysis, A Mathematical Approach*, 2.

4. For a very readable description of some of the early cryptographic and cryptanalytic techniques, see the first two chapters of Singh, *The Code Book*.

5. One of Dr. Shannon's (see chapter 5) contributions to information theory was showing that signals must be sampled at a rate at least twice that of the highest frequency component of the original signal that needed to be preserved.

## Appendix B. The Origins of NSA

1. The bulk of this material is extracted from the publication *The Origins of NSA* (see NSA Web site).

2. The Central Security Service (CSS) was established in 1972 by a presidential memorandum to provide a more unified cryptologic effort within the U.S. Department of Defense. As the chief of CSS, the director of NSA exercises control over the signals intelligence activities of the military services.

# GLOSSARY

This glossary contains brief definitions of some of the terms used in this book that may not be familiar to all readers. More detailed information is available in a variety of technical dictionaries.

**Algorithm.** A set of ordered steps for solving a problem such as a mathematical formula or the instructions in a software program.

**Alphanumeric data.** Data consisting of numbers mixed with alphabetic letters and special characters as in this glossary.

**Analog computer.** A device that processes infinitely varying signals, such as voltage. A thermometer is an example of a simple analog computer.

**Applications program.** Any software program that processes data for the user such as word processors and spreadsheets, as well as custom programs such as payroll, billing, design, and modeling and simulation.

**Bandwidth.** The capacity of a communications channel or circuit to transmit voice communications or data. The higher the bandwidth, the more data per second or the more simultaneous voice conversations can be transmitted.

**Binary arithmetic.** Arithmetic that uses numbers represented in binary form, that is, as sequences of zeros and ones.

**Bit.** A single digit in a binary number, that is, a zero or a one.

**Boolean algebra.** A deductive logical system usually applied to classes of things that are treated as algebraic quantities.

**Byte.** Eight bits, that is, eight zeros and/or ones. A byte is the common unit of computer storage. Bytes of data are used by computers to represent characters, such as numbers, letters, or typographical symbols.

**Calculus.** A mathematical theory developed by Sir Isaac Newton during his study of gravity to calculate the instantaneous velocity of an object moving between two points (e.g., an apple falling from a tree). The average velocity of the apple is calculated by dividing the distance it fell by the time it took to fall. The instantaneous velocity at any point in the fall is found by calculating the average velocity from this point to a very close point and then letting the close point get closer and closer; that is, the time required approaches zero in the limit. This calculation can be approximated, without taking the limit, with an algebraic approximation called the finite difference.

**Cathode ray tube (CRT).** A vacuum tube used for a computer display or television.

**Chips.** There are memory chips, microprocessor chips, and special-purpose chips for video games, automobiles, and watches among other consumer products. All consist of integrated circuits constructed on small semiconductor structures.

**Clock rate.** Often referred to as the clock cycle, this is the heart rate or tempo of the computer. The faster the clock speed, the faster the computer of a given word size. The clock rate is usually measured in MHz (megahertz, or millions of pulses per second).

**Compiler.** Software that translates a high-level programming language, such as C, into the computer's machine language. High-level programming languages are easier for programmers to use.

**Database.** A stored collection of data, nowadays electronically stored.

**Differential equation.** The mathematical expression that represents the relationship between the derivative and the independent variable is called a differential equation. The term *derivative* describes the change in one quantity with respect to another.

**Digital computer.** A computer that accepts and processes data that has been converted into binary numbers.

**Disk storage.** Disk storage (or hard disk) is a unit that stores data and provides the processor relatively quick access to large amounts of data, typically billions of bytes, on an electromagnetically charged surface or set of surfaces.

**Electromechanical binary computer.** A computer that uses binary arithmetic (representation of numbers by sequences of zeros and ones). The construction is of electromechanical parts, i.e., moving parts that are controlled by electricity. Printers are an example of an electromechanical device.

**File share.** The sharing of computer data in a computer network, often controlled by an administrator or passwords.

**Finite differences.** *See* calculus.

**Floating point operation.** A method of storing and calculating numbers in which the decimal points do not line up as in fixed point numbers but are represented as a separate unit called the exponent.

**Freeware.** Software that is offered free to the user. Shareware is software that is distributed free on the basis that the user may need or want to pay for it later.

**Frequency.** The number of times that a wave cycle (one peak and one trough) repeats in one second.

**Giga (G).** One billion.

**Gigabytes.** One billion bytes.

**Global disk memory.** The largest and slowest disk memory on a computer system in comparison to rapid-access disk memory or RAM. Used to store data not currently needed by the processor.

**Graphical display.** A display that utilizes graphics as well as characters or text. The familiar graphical user interface (GUI) with its icons and pull-down menus is an outgrowth of the invention of the graphical display and the mouse.

**Hacking.** Illegally gaining entrance to a computer system for unauthorized activities.

**Hertz (Hz).** Named after the German scientist Heinrich Hertz (1857–1894), the hertz is the unit of frequency for measuring the change of state, or cycle, in a cyclical waveform (sound, alternating electrical current, etc.). One hertz is one cycle per second.

**HF.** An abbreviation for "high frequency." A portion of the radio frequency spectrum generally defined as between 3 and 30 MHz.

**Integrated circuit.** A very small, very thin chip of silicon (or a material with similar characteristics) that contains millions of electronic components that perform various computer functions.

**Kilo (K).** One thousand.

**Magnetic drum memory.** An early high-speed computer storage device employing a magnetic-coated cylinder with tracks around its circumference. Each track had its own read/write head.

**Magnetic tape storage.** A sequential storage medium made of flexible plastic and organized on reels, cassettes, or cartridges. Nowadays, used primarily for data collection.

**Mega (M).** One million.

**Memory.** The holding place in the computer for instructions and data that the computer's processor can reach quickly. Today's memories are collections of RAM chips.

**Microprocessor.** The central processing unit (CPU) is the part of the computer that does the actual processing or computing (as opposed to storage or display for example). A microprocessor is a CPU that has been fabricated on a single, very small chip of silicon or other material.

**Microwave.** Radio frequencies above 1 gigahertz (1 GHz).

**Minicomputer.** A medium-size computer (as opposed to a mainframe) that functions as a single workstation or as a part of a multi-user system with up to several hundred terminals.

**Modulation.** Varying an electronic wave to transmit information. For example, one can vary the frequency of the wave (FM) or amplitude of the wave (AM).

**Object oriented (OO) programming language.** A programming language that supports the creation and processing of objects, software routines that function as independent building blocks that interact with one another.

**Operating system.** The master control program that runs the computer. It is the first program loaded into memory when the computer is turned on and its main part, the kernel, remains in main memory at all times.

**Packet switching.** A network switching technology that breaks up a message into smaller packets for transmission and switching purposes. This technology is the basis for the Internet and for local area networks within buildings or building complexes.

**Peripheral device.** Any hardware device connected to a computer, such as a monitor, keyboard, or printer.

**Predicate calculus.** The formal basis for the rules for establishing axioms and proving theorems from those axioms and the logical foundation for all mathematics.

**Program.** A collection of instructions that tell a computer what to do. The terms *program, instruction,* and *software* are often used interchangeably. When used as a verb, it refers to the act of writing instructions for a computer.

**Punch-card tabulating machine.** Punched cards are thin cardboard stock with eighty (usually) columns, each punched in a pattern signifying alphanumeric data. Processing of the cards was performed on separate machines for collating, sorting, calculating, etc.

**Quantum computing.** Computing that uses technology based on the principles of quantum theory (the theory that examines the nature and behavior of energy and matter at the atomic and subatomic level).

**Radio frequency.** The range of frequencies above the audio range and below visible light, from about 20 KHz to 300 GHz. All radio and television broadcasting is in this band of frequencies.

**Random access disk file.** Random access is the ability to go directly to a specific storage location on a disk without having to go through what's in front of it. *See* disk storage.

**Random access memory (RAM).** The RAM (also called main memory) is the place in the computer where the operating system, the application programs, and the data in current use are kept so they can be reached quickly by the computer's processor. Random means that each byte (eight bits) of data can be accessed in the memory without regard to the bytes before or after it.

**Realtime application.** An application that must respond immediately to changing conditions (e.g., space flight computers), or an application that must perform transactions fast enough to keep up with its real-world counterpart (e.g., transmitting live video).

**Reduced instruction set computer (RISC).** A computer design that reduces chip complexity by using simpler, and generally fewer, instructions.

**16-bit capability.** This capability refers to the number of bits in a computer word, the amount of data it can process at one time. The more bits in a word, the faster the computer can process data at a given clock rate.

**Semiconductor.** A solid substance that has physical properties between those of a conductor (easy flow of electricity) and an insulator (prevents the flow of electricity). When charged with electricity or light, semiconductors change from conductors to non-conductors, or vice versa. Their physical properties are fundamental to the field of solid-state electronics.

**Software.** A series of instructions for a computer. *See* program.

**Software compiler.** Software that translates a "higher-order" language used by programmers (e.g., COBOL or C) into machine language. Higher-order languages are easier for humans to use and understand but are not directly understood by the computer.

**Spectrum.** A range of electromagnetic frequencies.

**Switch.** In the communications system context, a switch is a network device that selects a path or circuit for sending voice or data to its next destination.

**System software.** Also called the "operating system," this is the software program that controls the computer itself, and it is used to control the operation of application programs and develop software (e.g., Windows, UNIX).

**Transistorized computer.** A computer built of transistorized components as opposed to vacuum tubes. The transistor is an on-off switch made of solid-state substances such as silicon. Transistors are more reliable than vacuum tubes, have a longer life, and use much less power.

**Two-address instruction.** A single computer instruction that performs an operation on data from two different locations in computer memory.

**UHF.** An abbreviation for "ultrahigh frequency." That portion of the radio frequency spectrum between 300 MHz and 1 GHz.

**Vacuum tube.** An electronic device that controls the flow of electrons in a vacuum. Used as on-off switches, they were the basis for the first digital computers. Today, they are primarily used in computer monitors and televisions.

**Vector processing.** Processing by a computer (vector processor) with built-in instructions that perform multiple calculations on vectors (one-dimensional arrays of numbers) simultaneously.

**VHF.** An abbreviation for "very high frequency." That portion of the radio frequency spectrum between 30 MHz and 300 MHz.

**Virtual memory.** Virtual memory simulates more main memory than actually exists by breaking a program up and storing parts on a disk and swapping them back and forth as required.

# BIBLIOGRAPHY

Akiera, Atsushi, and Frederik Nebeker. *From 0 to 1*. New York: Oxford University Press, 2002.

Bass, Michael, and Clayton Christensen. "The Future of the Microprocessor Business." *IEEE Spectrum* (April 2002): 34.

Bates, David Homer. *Lincoln in the Telegraph Office*. New York: Century, 1907.

Berlinski, David. *The Advent of the Algorithm*. New York: Harcourt, Inc., 2000.

Boone, J.V., and R. R. Peterson. *The Start of the Digital Revolution: SIGSALY, Secure Digital Voice Communications in World War II*. Fort Meade, MD: Center for Cryptologic History, National Security Agency, 2000.

Boyd, Carl. *Hitler's Japanese Confidant: General Oshima Hiroshi and MAGIC*. Lawrence: University of Kansas, 1993.

Brown, Julian. *The Quest for the Quantum Computer*. New York: Simon and Schuster, 2000.

Budianski, Stephen. *Battle of Wits*. New York: Free Press, 2000.

Burke, Colin. "An Introduction to a Historic Computer Document: The 1946 Pendergrass Report—Cryptanalysis and the Digital Computer." *Cryptologia*, vol. XVIII, no. 2 (April 1993).

Campbell, Joseph P. Jr., Thomas E. Tremain, and Vanoy C. Welch. "The Federal Standard 1016 4800 bps CELP Voice Coder." *Digital Signal Processing* 1, no. 3 (1991): 145–55.

Campbell-Kelly, Martin, and William Aspray. *A History of the Information Machine*. Sloan Technology Series, New York: Basic Books, 1997.

Clarke, Arthur C. "Extra-Terrestrial Relays. Can Rocket Stations Give Worldwide Radio Coverage?" *Wireless World* (October 1945): 305–8.

Crawford, David J., and Philip E. Fox. "The Autoscritcher and Superscritcher: Aids to Cryptanalysis of the German Enigma Cipher Machine, 1944–1946." *IEEE Annals of the History of Computing* 14, no. 3 (1992): 9–22.

Denning, Dorothy. *Cryptography and Data Security*. Reading, MA: Addison-Wesley Publishing Co., 1983.

Earley, M. H. *Family of Spies: Inside the John Walker Spy Ring*. New York: Bantam Books, reissue 1993.

Fishel, Edwin C. *The Secret War for the Union: The Untold Story of Military Intelligence in the Civil War*. Boston: Houghton Mifflin Co., 1996.

Friedman, Thomas L. *The Lexus and the Olive Tree: Understanding Globalization*. New York: Anchor Books, 2000.

Gebhard, Louis A. *Evolution of Naval Radio-Electronics and Contributions of the Naval Research Laboratory*. NRL Report 8300. Washington, DC: Naval Research Laboratory, 1979.

Gordon, John Steele. *A Thread Across the Ocean: The Heroic Story of the Transatlantic Cable*. New York: Walker & Co., 2002.

Haass, Richard N. "Supporting US Foreign Policy in the Post-9/11 World." *Studies in Intelligence* 46, no. 3 (2002).

Hagerman, Edward. Chapter 2 in *The American Civil War and The Origins of Modern Warfare*. Bloomington: Indiana University Press, 1988.

Hargrove, William, Forrest Hoffman, and Thomas Sterling. "Do-it-Yourself Supercomputer." *Scientific American* 265, no. 2 (2001): 72–79.

Hartmanis, Juris, and Herbert Lin, eds. *Computing the Future: A Broader Agenda for Computer Science and Engineering*. Washington, DC: National Academy Press, 1992.

Hecht, Jeff. *City of Light: The Story of Fiber Optics*. New York: Oxford University Press, 1999.

Hendry, John. *Innovating for Failure: Government Policy and the Early British Computer Industry*. Cambridge, MA: The MIT Press, 1990.

Ifrah, Georges. *The Universal History of Computing*. New York: John Wiley & Sons, 2001.

Johnson, George. *A Shortcut Through Time: The Path to the Quantum Computer*. New York: Alfred A. Knopf/Random House, 2003.

Kahn, David. *The Codebreakers*. New York: Scribner, 1996.

Kahn, Robert. "The Role of Government in the Evolution of the Internet," chapter 2 in *Revolution in the U.S. Information Infrastructure*. Washington, DC: National Academy of Sciences, 1994.

Kelly, Steve. *Big Machines*. Laguna Hills, CA: Aegean Park Press, 2001.

Kidwell, Peggy, and Paul Ceruzzi. *Landmarks in Digital Computing, A Smithsonian Pictorial History*. Washington, DC: Smithsonian Institution Press, 1994.

Klein, M. H. *Security for Record Communications: The TSC-KW-26*. Fort Meade, MD: Center for Cryptologic History, National Security Agency, 2002.

Levy, Steven. *Crypto*. New York: Viking Penguin, 2001.

Markle, Donald. *The Telegraph Goes to War: The Personal Diary of David Homer Bates, Lincoln's Telegraph Operator*. Hamilton, NY: Edmonston, 2003.

McCartney, Scott. *ENIAC*. New York: Berkley Books, 1999.

Meyer, Carl H., and Steven M. Matyas. *Cryptography*. New York: Wiley-Interscience, 1982.

Miller, A. Ray. *The Cryptographic Mathematics of Enigma*. Fort Meade, MD: Center for Cryptologic History, National Security Agency, 1999.

Miller, Francis Trevelyan, ed. *The Photographic History of the Civil War*, Vol. 8. New York: The Review of Reviews Co., 1912.

Morris, Richard B. *Encyclopedia of American History*. New York: Harper & Brothers, 1953.

Nichols, Randall. *ICSA Guide to Cryptography*. New York: McGraw-Hill, 1999.

Oppliger, Rolf. *Authentication Systems for Secure Networks*. Norwood, MA: Artech House, 1996.

Pecar, Joseph A., and David A. Garbin. *The New Telecom Factbook*. New York: McGraw-Hill, 2001.

Plum, William R. *The Military Telegraph During the Civil War in the United States*. Chicago: Jansen, McClurg and Co., 1882.

Postman, Neil. *Technopoly: The Surrender of Culture to Technology*. New York: Alfred A. Knopf, 1992.

Pugh, Emerson W., Lyle R. Johnson, and John H. Palmer. *IBM's 360 and Early 370 Systems*. Cambridge, MA: MIT Press, 1991.

Rappaport, Theodore S. *Wireless Communications: Principles and Practice*. Piscataway, NJ: IEEE Press, 1996.

Rojas, Raul, and Ulf Hashagen, eds. *The First Computers*. Cambridge, MA: MIT Press, 2000.

Rosenberg, Nathan, Ralph Landau, and David C. Mowery. *Technology and the Wealth of Nations*. Stanford, CA: Stanford University Press, 1992.

Rowlett, Frank B. *The Story of Magic*. Laguna Hills, CA: Aegean Park Press, 1998.

Schawlow, Arthur, and Charles Townes. "Infared and Optical Masers." *Physical Review* 112, December (1958): 1940–1949.

Schneier, Bruce. *Applied Cryptography*, second edition. New York: John Wiley & Sons, Inc., 1996.

Shannon, C. E. "Communication Theory of Secrecy Systems." *Bell Systems Technical Journal* 28 (October 1949): 656–715.

———. "A Mathematical Theory of Communications." *Bell Systems Technical Journal* 27 (July and October 1948): 379–423, 623–56.

Silverberg, Robert. *The Longest Voyage.* New York: The Bobbs-Merrill Co., 1972.

Simmons, Gustavus. *Contemporary Cryptology.* Piscataway, NJ: IEEE Press, 1992.

Singh, Simon. *The Code Book.* New York: Doubleday, 1999.

Sinkov, Abraham. *Elementary Cryptanalysis, A Mathematical Approach.* Washington, DC: Mathematical Association of America, 1966.

Smith, Michael. *Station X.* New York: TV Books, 1999.

Snyder, S.S. *Influence of the U.S. Cryptologic Organizations on the Digital Computer Industry.* (unpublished memo) Fort Meade, MD: National Security Agency, 1977.

Stafford, David. *Churchill and Secret Service.* Woodstock, NY: Overlook, 1998.

Stallings, William. *Network and Internet Security.* Piscataway, NY: IEEE Press, 1995.

Sterling, Thomas. "How to Build a Hypercomputer." *Scientific American* 285, no. 1 (2001): 38–45

Swade, Doron. *The Difference Engine: Charles Babbage and the Quest to Build the First Computer.* New York: Penguin Books, 2000.

Turing, Alan. *On Computable Numbers with an Application to the Entscheidungsproblem.* London: London Mathematical Society, 1937.

Urban, Mark. *The Man Who Broke Napoleon's Codes.* New York: Harper Collins, 2001.

Weber, Ralph E. *Masked Dispatches: Cryptograms and Cryptology in American History, 1775–1900.* United States Cryptologic History, Series I, Pre–World War I, Vol. I. Fort Meade, MD: Center for Cryptologic History, National Security Agency, 1993.

———. *United States Diplomatic Codes and Ciphers, 1775–1938.* Chicago: Precedent Publishing Inc., 1979.

Wilcox, Jennifer. *Solving the Enigma: History of the Cryptanalytic BOMBE.* Fort Meade, MD: Center for Cryptologic History, National Security Agency, 2002.

Williams, Kathleen Broome. *Grace Hopper: Admiral of the Cyber Sea.* Annapolis, MD: Naval Institute Press, 2004.

———. *Secret Weapon, U.S. High Frequency Direction Finding in the Battle of the Atlantic.* Annapolis, MD: Naval Institute Press, 1996.

Winter, Lumen, and Glenn Degner. *Minute Epics of Flight.* New York: Grosset and Dunlap, 1933.

## Organizational Publications

*Annual Report of the Smithsonian Institution for the Year Ending June 30, 1904.* Washington, DC: Government Printing Office, 1905.

*Balancing the National Interest.* (written by panels of the National Academy of Sciences, the National Academy of Engineering, and the Institute of Medicine) Washington, DC: National Academy Press, 1987.

*Eyewitness to the 20th Century.* Washington, DC: National Geographic Society, 1999.

*Federal Information Processing Standards Publication 46-2 (FPIS PUB 46-2).* Washington, DC: National Institute of Standards and Technology, December 30, 1993.

*History of Engineering and Science in the Bell Systems, National Service in War and Peace 1925–1975.* New York: Bell Telephone Laboratories, Inc., 1978.

*Museum Guide to the Heinz Nixdorf Museums Forum.* Paderborn, Germany: Heinz Nixdorf Museums Forum, 1999.

*Pioneers in U. S. Cryptology.* (brochure) Fort Meade, MD: Center for Cryptologic History, National Security Agency.

*United States Naval Aviation, 1910–60.* United States Navy, NavWeps 00–80P-1, CNO, 1960.

*U.S. Naval Cryptologic Veterans Association.* Paducah, KY: Turner Publishing Co., 1996.


## Web Sites

AT&T. www/att/cp/history/, "Technology and History of AT&T"

Bell Labs. www.bell-labs.com/history

Compaq. www5.compaq.com

The Computer Museum History Center. www.computerhistory.org

CyberStreet™ Internet solutions. www.cyberstreet.com/hcs/museum/chron.htm, "A Chronology of Computer History"

Defense Information Systems Agency. www-comm.itsi.disa.mil

History of Computing Project. www.thocp/hardware/

id Quantique. www.idquantique.com/company

IEEE. http://ieee.org, "Timeline of Computing History"

IEEE History Center. www.ieee.org/organizations/history_center

International Telecommunication Union. www.itu.int

Jerry Proctor. http://webhome.idirect.com/~jproc/crypto/

Motorola. www.Motorola.com/history, "Historical Timeline"

National Institute of Standards and Technology. http://museum.nist.gov

National Inventors Hall of Fame. www.invent.org

PBS. www.pbs.org/wgbh/amex, "The American Experience/The Telephone"

University of Mannheim, University of Tennessee, and National Energy Research
Scientific Computing Center. www.top500.org, "Top 500 Supercomputer
Sites"

U.S. Air Force public relations. www.af.mil/news/factsheets

U.S. Department of Justice. www.usdoj.gov, "Privacy Act Overview"

Virginia Polytechnic Institute and State University. http://ei.cs.vt.edu/~history/

# LIST OF CONTRIBUTORS

Assembling the data for and writing this work was a team effort. The primary team members all contributed in unique ways based on their personal experience in the field, as the following short biographical sketches illustrate.

Robert O. Alde received his bachelor of science degree in electronics engineering from the University of Illinois. While there, he was introduced to basic cryptology, which was part of the senior course in the U.S. Army Signal Corps' ROTC program. He was commissioned a second lieutenant at Ft. Monmouth in 1944 and assigned to Army Security Headquarters, Arlington Hall Station, Virginia, in the Signals Intelligence Systems Engineering Group. Upon the formation of the Armed Forces Security Agency (which later became the National Security Agency), he was assigned to the Research and Development organization as head of the Radio Frequency Research and Development Group. He also served as head of the Communication Security Research and Development Group and held many other engineering and management positions in the agency. After retiring in 1980 from federal service as NSA's assistant deputy director for research and engineering, Alde served as a consultant to industrial organizations on cryptology systems.

Albert E. Babbitt holds bachelor, master, and doctoral degrees in mathematics from Columbia University. Early in his career he was an instructor in the Mathematics Department of Rutgers University and a member of the technical staff of the U.S. Army Electronic Research and Development Laboratory at Ft. Monmouth, New Jersey. He joined IBM in the 1960s, leaving briefly to establish the System Engineering Office in the Defense Communications Agency for the Worldwide Military Command and Control System. He returned to IBM and held a series of senior management positions including vice president, technical staff, in IBM's Federal Systems Division, vice president and general manager of IBM's Gaithersburg, Maryland, operations, and vice president of space systems. Babbitt retired from IBM and joined TRW Inc.'s Systems and Integration Group, where he was vice president, requirements and group development. He retired from TRW in 1998 and is presently a consultant.

Robert E. Conley obtained a B.S. in electrical engineering from the University of Akron in 1959, an M.A. in applied mathematics from the University of Maryland in 1969, and a Ph.D. in computer science from George Washington University in 1971. He served on active duty in the U.S. Air Force from 1960 to 1963. In a varied and extensive government career, he has been an engineer and program manager at NSA (1963–74), the chief scientist of the U.S. Navy Command, Control, and Communications (1974–83), and the deputy assistant secretary, advanced technology and analysis, of the Department of the Treasury (1983–85). Conley has been the president of Conley & Associates, Inc., from 1985 to the present.

James J. Hearn received a bachelor of science degree in electrical engineering from Villanova University and was commissioned as a naval officer in 1959. He served five years in assignments as a surface naval warfare officer and as a design and test engineer in the U.S. Navy's nuclear propulsion program. Thereafter, he joined NSA and obtained a master's degree. In 1968, he completed a Ph.D. in electrical engineering at the Catholic University of America. In a thirty-four-year career at NSA, he held a variety of increasingly responsible positions: deputy director for information systems security (1988–94) and special U.S. liaison officer, U.S. Embassy, London, in the late 1990s. Hearn is now a part-time research adviser to students in Harvard University's Program on Information Resources Policy, and he also serves on the Board of Advisers of the Cyber Corps Program, which provides scholarships to advanced undergraduate and graduate students who are sponsored by the National Science Foundation and the Department of Defense.

Melville H. Klein joined the U.S. Army's Security Agency in 1948 after receiving his B.S. in electrical engineering from the University of Pittsburgh. His initial assignments were the design of secure communication and digital transmission systems. In 1954 he was awarded a graduate fellowship by NSA to Purdue, where he received a master's degree a year later. He returned to NSA as a design engineer and later spent a year at the Defense Communications Agency. Returning once more to NSA in 1963, Klein managed an R&D division. Subsequently, he was appointed to head the Office of Communication Security Research and Development and became the assistant deputy director for research and engineering. Still later, he served as the director of the Department of Defense's Computer Security Evaluation Center. Following his retirement in 1984, Klein joined IBM as a senior scientist until 1990. He currently volunteers at NSA's Center for Cryptologic History.

Thomas A. Prugh graduated from the University of Cincinnati and then served to the rank of captain in the U.S. Army Signal Corps during World War II. He worked for NSA and its predecessor agencies from 1946 to 1975, except for a stint in the 1950s when he was a research scientist at the National Bureau of Standards. Prugh held many technical and management positions at NSA including serving as the head of the national cryptologic school. In addition to his personal contributions in digital microelectronics, he was actively engaged in the applications of minicomputers to many problems including those of home management. He retired from NSA in 1975 as the assistant director for science and technology and went to work for the Institute for Defense Analysis until his second retirement in 1986.

# INDEX

Italicized page numbers indicate illustrations or photos.

179

# ABOUT THE AUTHOR

James V. Boone obtained a bachelor's degree in electrical engineering from Tulane University in 1955 and a master's degree in that discipline from the U.S. Air Force Institute of Technology in 1959. He entered active duty with the Air Force in 1955 and served to the rank of captain, with tours in the Air Research and Development Command and the Air Force Security Service. Assigned by the latter to NSA, he worked as a design engineer until he converted to civilian status in late 1962.

Boone then held a variety of engineering and management positions at NSA and resigned in early 1981 to join TRW Inc. At that time he was NSA's deputy director for research and engineering. His career at TRW involved both management and staff positions and included serving as the vice president and general manager of the Electronic Systems Group in Redondo Beach, California. He retired from TRW in 1996. Subsequently, he has been an adjunct professor at George Mason University and the Joint Military Intelligence College.

**The Naval Institute Press** is the book-publishing arm of the U.S. Naval Institute, a private, nonprofit, membership society for sea service professionals and others who share an interest in naval and maritime affairs. Established in 1873 at the U.S. Naval Academy in Annapolis, Maryland, where its offices remain today, the Naval Institute has members worldwide.

Members of the Naval Institute support the education programs of the society and receive the influential monthly magazine *Proceedings* and discounts on fine nautical prints and on ship and aircraft photos. They also have access to the transcripts of the Institute's Oral History Program and get discounted admission to any of the Institute-sponsored seminars offered around the country.

The Naval Institute also publishes *Naval History* magazine. This colorful bimonthly is filled with entertaining and thought-provoking articles, first-person reminiscences, and dramatic art and photography. Members receive a discount on *Naval History* subscriptions.

The Naval Institute's book-publishing program, begun in 1898 with basic guides to naval practices, has broadened its scope to include books of more general interest. Now the Naval Institute Press publishes about one hundred titles each year, ranging from how-to books on boating and navigation to battle histories, biographies, ship and aircraft guides, and novels. Institute members receive significant discounts on the Press's more than eight hundred books in print.

Full-time students are eligible for special half-price membership rates. Life memberships are also available.

For a free catalog describing Naval Institute Press books currently available, and for further information about subscribing to *Naval History* magazine or about joining the U.S. Naval Institute, please write to:

Customer Service
**U.S. Naval Institute**
291 Wood Road
Annapolis, MD 21402-5034
Telephone: (800) 233-8764
Fax: (410) 269-7940
Web address: www.navalinstitute.org